SIN
Biblical Perspectives
by Eugene H. Maly

Pflaum/Standard
Cincinnati, Ohio 45231

Excerpts from the *New American Bible*
© 1970 used herein by permission
of the Confraternity of Christian
Doctrine, copyright owner.

ISBN: 0-8278-0006-1
Library of Congress Catalog
Card Number: 73-79518
Published by Pflaum/Standard

Nihil Obstat
Ralph A. Asplan
Censor Deputatis

Imprimatur
† Joseph L. Bernardin
Archbishop of Cincinnati

January 31, 1973

10006/4.8M/S8M-2-1273

Contents

Preface

The following pages are a much expanded form of an article on sin that appeared originally in the *Catechist*. The author is grateful to the editor, Rod Brownfield, for his encouragement and helpful suggestions in completing the study that appears here, although the former must take responsibility for any deficiencies.

This is not a scholarly presentation in the strict sense, even though it is based on sound biblical scholarship. It is intended for the interested Christian—both the one who is involved in any way in the formation of the young as parent, catechist or religious educator, and the one who simply wishes to have a better grasp of what the Scriptures have to say about the reality of sin in its many aspects. As Christians, we believe that, while the Bible does not provide us with ready answers to all modern problems of religion, it is the foundation on which all succeeding revelation rests. What it has to say, therefore, forms a necessary framework within which all religious questions are formulated and, in varying degrees, are answered. This is as true of the question of sin as of any other.

After an initial observation on the contemporary attitude toward sin, the study considers what is basic to the biblical concept, namely, its relationship to the living God. A brief treatment of the biblical terms used for sin is offered then to show the nature of sin as progressively understood by the biblical authors. Next, one of the more important dimensions of sin is considered, that is, its covenant or social structure. This is important especially in our day because of the dangers of extreme individualism. There follows the notion of sin as including, in a much greater way than usually thought, the failure to act when action or involvement is required.

The following dimensions are taken up in turn. The biblical treatment of lists of "objective" sins will throw some light on the perennial question of detailed lists. The problem of degrees of sin at times has been treated in an overly simplified way; it must be asked whether there is a biblical foundation for what we traditionally have called "mortal" and "venial" sins. Another failure in some catecheses of sin has been the tendency to emphasize individual sinful actions to the exclusion of—or at least covering over of—the more fundamental "state of sin." The biblical realism also is shown in its description of sin as a power in the world.

Does God punish the sinner? The question is asked today with increasing intensity. There can be no doubt that the Bible associates punishment with sin, but there was a development in the understanding of that association. And, ultimately, it is seen that the sinner judges himself, possibly in a definitive manner. The vexing problem of evil in the world is discussed briefly in its relation to sin. And original sin is examined in relation to the whole mystery of sin.

More positively, the study considers the victory won over sin by Jesus Christ and the various ways in which the New Testament describes that victory. Finally, there is a treatment of the sinner's conversion and of the necessity of forgiveness of others.

The author is very much aware of the many limitations of his presentation. First, while it is hoped that the more important aspects of sin are considered here, there are other, perhaps more peripheral, aspects that are not. Also, those aspects that are considered could have been developed in much greater depth. In both cases, however, it was felt that the ultimate purpose of the study, which is to provide a handy guide to the biblical notion of sin, would have been defeated. Again, the reader may be disappointed in not finding here all the contemporary moral applications of the aspects of sin that are studied. But that, too, would have exceeded both the purpose of the presentation and the competence of the author. Finally, there is what might be called the limitation of negativity. Reading page after page about sin well may evoke a sense of morbidity. This limitation, unfortunately, is inherent in the subject itself; it is difficult to find anything happy to say about sin, unless it be sin's defeat, and we do speak about that.

With these limitations in mind, we offer this study to our readers in the hope that a better understanding of the reality of sin will produce a more realistic attitude in our relationship to God and to the world and, ultimately, a more concerted effort to achieve that *shalom* whose only enemy is sin.

Eugene H. Maly

SIN
Biblical Perspectives

Contemporary Attitudes

High on the list of unpopular theological language these days are such terms as angels, devils, miracles, judgment, hell and sin. The list could be extended, but the point is made. The theologian who attempts to discuss these concepts is confronted with a man-centered theology that takes its departure not from a revelation from on high but from the human situation as it is in the world today. Such a theology does not take kindly to unworldly beings, to interventions from without or to the possibility of ultimate human failure.

But why the unpopularity of sin? Sin would seem to be part of the human condition that meets everyone in life. If sin is an evil, then it would seem that only the extreme optimist—or the extreme pessimist— would refuse to accept its existence. Actually, sin's unpopularity lies not in the refusal to accept evil or imperfection but in the refusal to call it "sin." Sin traditionally implies moral perversion and guilt, and these terms in turn imply a personal aversion from a transcendent Being to whom man is responsible and because of whom guilt is possible. In other words, sin has been defined, in the Christian tradition, as affecting the relationship between man and God. Thus the more at ease we are with the idea of a personal God the more readily we can accept the reality of sin. To accept sin, man must *believe* in sin, since faith alone can accept the kind of God against whom man can sin. Outside the context of faith, sin has no meaning; it is reduced to a necessary imperfection in the upward sweep of human evolution.

A concomitant factor in the modern disaffection with sin is the overly juridical or legalistic manner in which it was presented in the catechesis of the past. Closely reasoned distinctions between material and formal sin, mortal and venial sin, the exhaustive listing of categories of sins—all of these have tended to produce boredom in the person who seeks, if only subconsciously, a vital response to man's fumbling quest for God. An interesting comparison could be made between the older textbooks of moral theology with their minute distinctions between what is permissible and not permissible on Sunday and the ancient Mishna of Judaism with its equally minute observations on what constituted a violation of the Sabbath. In both cases, the broader context of faith in a living God seems to have been missed. And thus the distinctions have been drained of life and, ultimately, of meaning.

Finally, on a deeper philosophical level, there are those who reject the notion that man is capable of failure, especially of ultimate failure. This is the position of those who recognize only a constant progression in man's conquest of the world and of himself. The technological advances of modern man have conditioned them to think only in terms of betterment, of the inevitable thrust towards utopia. For them, it is inconceivable that man, even individual man, could fail in the effort. Basically, this position reduces itself to a denial of human freedom, for that which cannot *not* be achieved is not achieved freely.

Biblical religion takes sin seriously. Indeed, sin is the one factor that makes sense of the divine activity in the world of man. If Jesus Christ is the climactic revelation of God, then the reason for His coming tells us something significant about biblical religion. John the Baptist defines Jesus in these terms, "Look! There is the Lamb of God who takes away the sin of the world!" (John 1:29). Jesus Himself accepted this designation, when at the Last Supper, He referred to the contents of the cup as ". . . my blood, the blood of the covenant, to be poured out in behalf of many for the forgiveness of sins" (Matthew 26:28). While the plural form of the word in the Matthean text would suggest the particular sins of individual men, the singular noun used by the Baptist summarizes all sin as directed against the saving activity of God, as the ultimate weapon used by the power of evil in the world.

We hope to present in what follows some of the major aspects of sin as they are presented in the Scriptures. While this survey would not presume to provide an exhaustive catechesis of sin, it is basic to any such catechesis. It is with biblical revelation that we must begin, not with the metaphysical principles of some philosophy. It is in the Scriptures that we meet the living Word whose "study is, as it were, the soul of sacred theology" (Vatican Council II, *Revelation*, #24).

Sin and the Living God

Sin in the Bible, as already intimated, is first and foremost a breach of the relationship between man and God. For this reason, religion and morality, or ethics, are not seen as distinct aspects of human activity. Rather, morality is seen always within the broad framework of man's relationship to God, or as an aspect of religion. This view is in distinct contrast to the classical Greek view that could conceive of ethical behavior in terms that had no religious connotations whatever. Absolutely basic to an understanding of biblical religion and morality is an awareness of the personal, self-revealing God against whom all sin is directed. We shall consider some of the evidence for this as found in the Scriptures.

Perhaps the clearest statement on this religious character of sin is found in the well-known Psalm, *Miserere*, where the author cries out to God, "Against you only have I sinned, and done what is evil in your sight" (Psalm 51:6). The psalmist is describing the reaction of David to his double offense against Bath-sheba and Uriah (cf. 2 Samuel 11). In dialectical fashion, it is said to be a sin against God alone, not because injustice was not done to the man and his wife, but because the religious element of any sin is sufficient to describe its true horror. Even in the prose account of David's sin and his repentance, he is said to confess to the prophet Nathan, "I have sinned against the Lord" (2 Samuel 12:13).

If sin is primarily and always an offense against God, then the greatest sin would be the direct rejection of the true God as Lord and the consequent setting up of false gods, or idols, in His place. This was *the* sin par excellence in the Old Testament, where the temptation to do so was greatly abetted by the practices of Israel's pagan neighbors. The rejection of the true God and the carving of idols are the first offenses mentioned in the famous Decalogue given to the people through Moses. And it is instructive to note that, in the context of this evil, God is said to inflict punishment on "those who hate me" (Exodus 20:5). Here sin is depicted most forcefully as hatred of God.

In the light of this biblical view, we can say that the faith context is an absolute "given" when approaching the roots of a theology of sin in the Bible. It might even be said that the greatest sin is not to accept sin, because not to accept sin is to reject the One because of whom sin is possible. The Bible expresses this as rejecting the living God and setting up idols that can be manipulated by man into condoning and even fostering man's evil inclinations. Against all our idols, there can be no sin, for in idols there is no jealousy for man. The Old Testament writers could picture sin as an offense against God because they could conceive of God as jealous for man (Exodus 20:5).

In the Gospels, we find no reference to idols or idolatry, principally because they were written for those who already had accepted God and Jesus Christ as Son and Savior. But in the letters of Paul, which reveal a contact with the pagan inhabitants of the Mediterranean world, the concern of idolatry is manifest. In his epistle to the Romans, Paul uses especially strong terms to express the sin of the pagans who had a sufficient knowledge of God to make their rejection of Him culpable. Since God had made His existence clear to them through the things He has made, "Therefore these men are inexcusable" (1:20).

We stress this point only to show that, in biblical religion, morality is inconceivable outside the context of religion. Rejection of God is *the* sin against which all sin is measured. In modern Western society, idolatry as practiced in the ancient world is hardly the same danger that it was then. The Second Vatican Council has shown that even those who profess atheism or agnosticism may not be rejecting the transcendent Lord but only rejecting the concept of God as they see Him revealed in the lives of so-called Christians. Still, the basic biblical conviction remains valid. If sin is an offense against God, then outright rejection of God must be the greatest sin.

We find in the first letter of John another clear expression of this relationship of sin to God. The author first defines the revelation of God as directed to the removal of sin: "You know well that the reason he revealed himself was to take away sins; in him there is nothing sinful" (1 John 3:5). It follows, then, that the one who accepts God does not sin, and the one who sins separates himself from God. "The man who remains in him does not sin. The man who sins has not seen him or known him" (3:6).

The Vocabulary of Sin

When we examine the terms used for sin in the Bible, we will realize more sharply the relationship of sin to God, and we will be provided with an introduction to other aspects of this reality. While it is true that our English word "sin" almost exclusively is seen in an ethico-religious sense, thus always suggesting an offense against God, Israel had to borrow her vocabulary for sin from her experience of human relations. So at times we may find the words used in a religiously neutral sense. But this usage permits us to have a deeper understanding of their meaning when applied to the divine-human relationship.

The most commonly used verb in the Scriptures for sinning could be translated properly as "missing the mark." The author of Proverbs uses the word in a neutral sense when he writes, "It is not good for a man to be without knowledge, and he who makes haste with his feet misses the way" (19:2; *Revised Standard Version* translation). When used in a moral sense, it immediately could conjure up visions of codes of law, of legal formulae that must be observed in all their minute details. Such legalism was in fact a real danger in later Judaism when an excessive concern for recording and observing all the legal prescriptions of the past manifested itself.

But in the Old Testament "missing the mark" primarily was not failing to fulfill the letter of the law; it was failing to conform to the covenant relationship that God had established between Himself and Israel. Here is a wider dimension that lifts sin out of its legalistic morass to set it on the level of man's life with God. To sin is not simply to break a rule; it is to fail to respond to the love of Another.

A perfect illustration of this breach of covenant love is found in Deuteronomy. The author describes the scene in which Moses descends from the Mount, where Yahweh has delivered to him the laws governing the covenant relationship, to find the people worshipping the golden calf. In the zeal of the moment, Moses exclaimed, "I saw how you had sinned against the Lord, your God: you had already turned aside from the way which the Lord had pointed out to you by making for yourselves a molten calf!" (9:16). In their sin, the Israelites completely missed the mark of that love whereby God had committed Himself to them. Moses' destruction of the two tablets symbolized the breach of the covenant relationship, the underlying reality that gave the whole meaning to the Ten Commandments. It was not just that Israel had "broken a commandment"; she had broken a personal bond of which the commandment was but the external expression.

Much of Israel's vocabulary of sin, as well as that of the New Testament, is colored by this notion of covenant. There were covenants—or pacts, or treaties—between individuals, such as between David and Jonathan (cf. 1 Samuel 18:3); but the covenants that decisively influenced the theology of sin were covenants between God and the people. While they may have been mediated by individuals, such as Moses, they always were established with the people or nation. Later we shall see an important consequence of this factor. What is important for our purposes now is that the whole idea of covenant presupposes God's preliminary choice of Israel as His people. There is no basis within the people itself for this choice; it proceeds from the unsolicited love of God. In the moving language of the Deuteronomist, "It was not because you are the largest of all nations that the Lord set his heart on you and chose you, for you are really the smallest of all nations. It was because the Lord loved you and because of his fidelity to the oath he had sworn to your fathers, that he brought you out with his strong hand from the place of slavery . . ." (7:7-8).

God positively expressed His unsolicited love in His mighty act of saving His people from slavery, which, in turn, demanded a response on the part of the people. The covenant is the description of God's saving love and the spelling out of Israel's response. In the covenant, there is no prescription of God's obligations; His faithfulness, from the very beginning, is presupposed. Indeed, the whole covenant theology is built on this absolute foundation of God's *hesed* (covenant love or loving kindness). This love demands a response on the part of Israel, a response of faithfulness that is manifested externally in the stipulations that make up the covenant code. Obeying these commandments, therefore, is far more than an act of legal conformism; it is an act of covenant faithfulness, an interior response of loyalty to One who first has expressed the act of love; it finds its necessary external expression in certain obligations. Basically, then, sin is the violation of this relationship, the rejection of this love. Thus, we can understand why the Deuteronomist should describe the act of worship of the golden calf as "missing the mark" of that love that God had just manifested to them.

If sin basically is a failure to love God, it is not surprising that it should be associated so frequently with the heart. For the biblical authors, the heart is associated with various emotional and intellectual activities. It is the arena of man's life with God, of his response to God. To sin, then, is to harden the heart to God's love, expressed in covenant; it is to deny the heart its proper role. ". . . this people draws near with words only, and honors me with their lips alone, though their hearts are far from me . . ." (Isaiah 29:13). "Cleanse your heart of evil, O Jerusalem, that you may be saved" (Jeremiah 4:14).

In the Psalm already referred to, David is pictured as beseeching God not to spurn a heart that has been broken by the guilt and punishment of sin (51:19) and to create a clean heart for him that will not be defiled again by sin (51:12). Jeremiah, in an especially illustrative passage, speaks about the new covenant that God will make with His people. Like the old covenant, it will be responded to by moral conduct expressed in covenant law. But unlike the old covenant, the law of the new covenant will be written in the people's heart so that all will know, almost instinctively, right from wrong. "I will place my law within them, and write it upon their hearts; I will be their God, and they shall be my people. No longer will they have need to teach their friends and kinsmen how to know the Lord. All, from least to greatest, shall know me, says the Lord, for I will forgive their evildoing and remember their sin no more" (31:33-34).

The common word for "sin" in the Bible, then, clearly envisions a relationship of love between God and man that has been violated. Thus to speak of sin in a purely social context—as though social injustice were sin in and by itself—is to distort the biblical meaning. This sense appears to be intended more explicitly in another term used to express sin. Although it usually is translated "transgression" or "offense," its non-religious usage would suggest the translation "rebellion." Thus in 1 Kings 12:19, the northern kingdom of Israel is said to have rebelled against Judah. There is a personal relationship implied since the northern tribes are rebelling against their brother tribes. Also involved in the word is a wilful or deliberate act of the one committing the rebellion.

All these implications may not be intended in all instances of the use of the word, but it is the surface meaning of many texts. For example, when Isaiah complains that the people of Judah, who had been raised as sons by Yahweh, now rebel against Him (1:2), the image obviously is that of a personal relationship that is violated. And the deliberateness of the act of rebellion is brought out by Amos when he tells Israel, "Come to Bethel and sin, to Gilgal, and sin the more . . ." (4:4). The irony of the invitation does not lessen the imperious attitude against God that is implied.

Some modern authors are so struck by the wilfulness of this action against God that they refer to the "numinous" character of sin. This means what we have been insisting on here, namely, that sin is "a spontaneous human reaction to the holy and the divine" (Quell). This is why the prophets, all of whom had a keen sense of the transcendence or holiness of God, were so appalled by the callous behavior of the people. The very fact that God is involved makes the rebellion of sin the unique act that it is.

Our examination of these two words used for sin in the Hebrew Testament is sufficient to expose what is distinctive of the biblical doctrine of sin. In the Hellenistic world, it was not the moral will of God that was involved but a certain measure that could be discovered in nature. Thus, a study of nature could suffice to distinguish between right and wrong. In the Scriptures, on the other hand, it always is the holy God who is involved, and His will is the ultimate norm for morality. This is what makes the book of Job, for example, the great literary drama that it is. When biblical man cannot find in himself the evidences of rebellion against God, he must engage in contest with God Himself to find an explanation for the apparent consequences of sin.

Even though the New Testament vocabulary of sin is not as rich as that of the Hebrew Bible, the dominant note of opposition to God is present still. In fact, it often is presented as a personified power, especially by St. Paul. Both Jews and Greeks "are under the domination of sin" (Romans 3:9), and what this means the apostle spells out clearly when he says that "the whole world stands convicted before God" (Romans 3:19); all are "God's enemies" (Romans 5:10). In the New Testament, we can see a drama being enacted between this power of sin and the Kingdom of God, represented by Jesus Christ. "You were dead because of your sins and offenses, as you gave allegiance to the present age, that spirit who is even now at work among the rebellious . . . But God is rich in mercy; because of his great love for us he brought us to life with Christ when we were dead in sin. By this favor you were saved" (Ephesians 2:1-2, 4-5). Again, in the biblical view, if sin is not against God, it is not sin.

Sin's Social Dimension

When sin is viewed as a violation of covenant love, its social dimension immediately emerges. Thus, while the core meaning of sin is to be found in its relationship to God, the decisive and external criterion of morality is relationship to others (P. Ricoeur): God's covenant is made not with individuals but with the community. *Israel* is God's people, and individuals are affected inasmuch as they belong to the community. Moreover, any action of an individual Israelite has its repercussions on the covenanted people. A vivid, if excessive, illustration of this sense of community is given in the early practice of punishing an entire family for the sin of one of its members. The Israelite army had been unsuccessful in one of its battles, and it was decided that the sin of one of its members was responsible for the guilt of the entire community. Accordingly, the culprit, together with his family, was stoned to death (Joshua 7).

Later prophets emphasized individual responsibility

in the matter of sin: "For all lives are mine; the life of the father is like the life of the son, both are mine (says the Lord); only the one who sins shall die" (Ezekiel 18:4). But this emphasis did not remove the covenant implications from the act of sin. Sin, even if committed alone, weakened the community since it affected the relationship with Yahweh, Lord of the people. There are no "private" sins, in the strict sense of that word.

This concept explains the special denunciation that the prophets made against kings and priests and other members of the "establishment." These leaders embodied the community in a special way, and hence their crimes affected the community even more seriously than did those of other individuals. "Woe to the shepherds who mislead and scatter the flock of my pasture, says the Lord. Therefore, thus says the Lord, the God of Israel, against the shepherds who shepherd my people: You have scattered my sheep and driven them away. You have not cared for them, but I will take care to punish your evil deeds" (Jeremiah 23: 1-2).

The conviction of a community dimension of sin carried over into Christianity. There, too, the covenant relationship, sealed now through the blood of Jesus Christ, formed the foundation for the concept of the Christian community. Paul developed this concept in his theology of the body of Christ, with all the repercussions that has on the mutual relationships between members. Perhaps nowhere does he betray this deep, underlying conviction of the social consequences of sin more than when he urges the Christian community to expel one of its incestuous members: "Do you not know that a little yeast has its effect all through the dough? Get rid of the old yeast . . ." (1 Corinthians 5:1-8).

We cannot stress too much this communal dimension of sin in our day, when an excessive individualism is threatening to undermine morality. Individual rights are being championed as the supreme, if not exclusive, goals of man, and individual consciences as the sole criteria for ethical conduct. Anyone acquainted with the arguments of those who want "abortion on demand" can bear witness to this form of individualism that vitiates the social nature of man. And yet, as one author has put it, "An awareness of the concrete, essential unity of the whole family of Adam belongs to the most fundamental data of the Bible . . ." (L. Scheffczyk). Thus, any contemporary catechesis of sin must be alert to this challenge to Christian morality and must be prepared to meet it with constant stress on the social or communitarian dimension of every aspect of Christian doctrine, including that of sin.

On the positive side of this social dimension of biblical morality, we can note the constant prophetic insistence on concern for others. One of the strongest prophetic condemnations of a falsely motivated cultic religion is found in the book of Isaiah. The prophet first severely warns the people of Jerusalem that worship alone does not guarantee salvation. He does so in a way that might lead the reader to think that he is against cultic worship altogether: "What care I for the number of your sacrifices? says the Lord. I have had enough of whole-burnt rams and fat of fatlings; In the blood of calves, lambs and goats I find no pleasure. When you come in to visit me, who asks these things of you? Trample my courts no more! Bring no more worthless offerings; your incense is loathsome to me" (1:11-13). But the absoluteness of these reproofs only serves to highlight the real wickedness of the people. Their worship of God is absolutely worthless—not because God is not to be worshipped but because it is not accompanied by concern for the fellowman. "Your hands are full of blood! Wash yourselves clean! Put away your misdeeds from before my eyes; cease doing evil; learn to do good. Make justice your aim: redress the wronged, hear the orphan's plea, defend the widow" (1:15-16).

What is implied, if not yet explicated, in this remarkable passage is that there must be an interior bond between religion, which deals with our relationship to God, and morality, which deals with our relationship to our neighbor. They are not two separate categories of the human condition, acting independently of one another. The one is radically affected by the other—a point that is brought out by Isaiah's dialectic of condemning the one that is not accompanied by the other.

Jesus of Nazareth first made this association explicit when He summed up the whole of morality in the twofold commandment of love of God and love of neighbor (cf. Mark 12:28-31). The implications of this unity are enormous. It excludes any kind of supposed relationship to God in an isolated form; it demands that love of God be manifested in love of man. By insisting on love, Jesus interiorizes the Isaian condemnations, which, as described, are acts of justice. This New Testament unification of love of God and of neighbor is formulated in a very practical way by St. John when he writes, "One who has no love for the brother he has seen cannot love the God he has not seen" (1 John 4:20).

There is somewhat common agreement today on the necessity of love of neighbor shown in a practical way by acts of charity. The danger seems to be that this is identified actually with love of God. Since the one who truly is open to others necessarily is open to God, it might be argued that there need be no expression of love of God. But this position would be confusing the evidence of love of God with its substance. Jesus formulated both commandments, and in His preaching, the love of God always takes precedence. The basic reason for this is that, just as in sin, so in love of God, there is a "numinous" element that makes it categorically different from love of neighbor. To love the transcendent Lord requires an act of total surrender that could not be demanded in any other love. To identify love of God completely with love of neighbor would be to destroy this element in love and would reduce God to " a mere term and cipher, which one will soon manage to do without" (G. Bornkamm). Thus, in the Christian dispensation, love of God becomes the necessary presupposition and adequate foundation for love of neighbor.

Would it be correct to say that biblical revelation

was an early champion of what we know today as social justice? If social justice is understood as some kind of social system or expression of a particular brand of political socialism, then the Scriptures know nothing of it. Biblical religion and biblical morality transcend all specific systems, whether social, political or economic. But if social justice is taken in the broad sense of concern for all men, regardless of distinctions, then obviously it is at the heart of revealed religion.

Indeed, the biblical concept of justice has a distinct, even unique, character inasmuch as justice towards man is an emergent of man's love of God. That is why a sin against justice is sin, in the biblical view, precisely because it is, first of all, a rejection of God. Just as there is a profound unity in man's love of God and of his fellowman, so is there a similar unity in man's refusal to love God and man.

Sin as Nonaction

Included in the biblical view of sin is the failure to act when action is demanded. We are acquainted with this aspect of sin under the traditional heading of "sins of omission." Moral theologians today are recognizing that, in the past, these sins have not been emphasized sufficiently. Avoiding evil action was thought to be the near exclusive concern of morality. Performing acts of charity or justice, for society at large, was felt to be a social or political, not primarily a religious, concern. There was, at least, a tendency in this direction.

But biblical religion, in conjunction with its command to love and to serve God, sees as a necessary concomitant the command to love and to serve the other. Failure to do so—the attitude of noninvolvement —is the object of biblical censure. We saw Isaiah's condemnation of his people for their failure to redress the wrongs of others. Even the most meticulous practice of ritual worship does not absolve one from these "sins of omission." Among the crimes for which Amos condemned the luxury-loving Israelites was "repelling the needy at the gate," failing to look on poverty and to alleviate it.

Two examples from the prophets especially are illustrative of the temptation to noninvolvement and of the price that must be paid for involvement. Amos was a shepherd from the scrubby hills of Judah when he was called to carry God's word to the northern kingdom of Israel. It was a hard word that he had to bring to the people, and it earned him only the enmity of the king and the denunciation of the priest Amaziah. But as Amos replied to the priest, "I was no prophet, nor have I belonged to a company of prophets; I was a shepherd and a dresser of sycamores. The Lord took me from following the flock, and said to me, Go, prophesy to my people Israel" (Amos 7:14-15). Amos would have had good reason for refusing the call, but he realized that it would have been a "sin of omission."

The case of Jeremiah was similar. When called by God to prophesy destruction to the people of Judah, he protested that he was too young, that he did not know how to speak (Jeremiah 1:6). But the call was from the Lord, and the young man did as he was commanded. The price he had to pay for his involvement is brought out in one of his bitter "confessions:" "You duped me, O Lord, and I let myself be duped; you were too strong for me, and you triumphed. All the day I am an object of laughter; everyone mocks me . . . The word of the Lord has brought me derision and reproach all the day" (20:7-8). This interior crisis was the result of his refusal to commit the sin of nonaction.

24

The best example of this biblical concern is found in Jesus' parable of the good Samaritan. The main point of the parable is not to indicate that every man, regardless of differences, is our neighbor—which is brought out, of course, by the fact that a Samaritan aided a Jew. Rather, the main point is to show that love of neighbor consists in positive action in his favor. The priest and the Levite are contrasted with the Samaritan, not primarily inasmuch as they are Jews, but inasmuch as they fail to act. This is clear from the manner in which Jesus turns the question of the lawyer around, changing the point from a consideration of the object of good acts to a consideration of the subject of good acts. Note that, while the lawyer asks Jesus, "And who is my neighbor?" Jesus replies with the parable and concludes with the question, "Which of these three . . . was a neighbor to the man who fell in with the robbers?" (Luke 10:29-36). The law of charity is universalized by Jesus, not by an exhaustive listing of all possible neighbors, but by the expedient of putting the emphasis on the man who acts. According to the parable, a neighbor is not a human being existing somewhere in the world; a neighbor is one who acts as neighbor. Sin, in this case, is failure to act as neighbor.

Sin and Objective Actions

According to the new morality, the only absolute principle is to love. While we have no intention of discussing all the complexities posed by this position, we can note that, on the popular level, there is a fear that there are no more objective moral standards and that no actions can be proposed as outright sinful. In the catechesis of sin, this could result in refusing to mention, for example, the Ten Commandments or to accept any objective sinful actions. While it is a sound principle of morality to stress the positive role of Christian virtue and the need for growing maturely in love (this is, in effect, what Jesus Himself did when He answered the question about the "great commandment"), the Bible frequently does propose lists of sins that are to be avoided. It would be false to a biblical theology of sin to ignore these altogether.

First, it would be wrong to think that any list of sins in the Scriptures was intended as an exhaustive set of principles that were sufficient to guide the Israelite or

Christian in his moral life. Even the Ten Commandments were proposed only as basic minimum requirements that flowed from the covenant relationship with
Yahweh. Besides, analysis of the Decalogue has shown
that it underwent much development in its long history
within Israel. Certainly no absolute moral code was
expected to be derived from it.

The listing of sins to be avoided was a frequent exercise of the biblical authors in their concern for a faith-
centered morality. Thus, Ezekiel gives a catalogue of
twelve actions that define the virtuous man (18:5-9)
and another list of six evil deeds committed by the
people of Judah (33:25-26). Amos lists the crimes of
various nations, including Judah and Israel (1-2). In
Deuteronomy, the Levites are told to proclaim a series
of curses for twelve crimes that are to be avoided
(27:15-26). And the psalmist provides a kind of
"pocket list" of moral values that the one who wishes
to enter the Lord's sanctuary should possess (Psalm
15).

In the New Testament, there are similar lists of sins,
with the Decalogue of Moses retaining its validity in
the eyes of Jesus. In fact, the passage in which the rich
young man asks Jesus for the way to eternal life and
in which Jesus replies with a modified form of the
Decalogue (Mark 10:17-19) is a bit incongruous in
the face of Jesus' usual call to faith and conversion.
That the Evangelist has recorded it suggests that it still
was considered good pedagogy in the Christian church.
The Ten Commandments have as much validity for
Christians as they had for Israel, even if they now are

seen in a new dimension or context.

All the lists of sins to which we have referred so far are historically conditioned. That is, while some of them will have at least a relative validity for all time because they affect the very nature of man, still the manner in which they were formulated and the concerns reflected in the listing itself are determined by the historical situation. A catechesis of sin, therefore, would not simply gather together all the lists of sins in the Bible and propose them as valid today in the same way that they were then. A consideration of the historical background would have to be made. Thus, while the carving of idols is as wrong today as it was at the time of Moses (cf. Exodus 20:4-5), the modern catechist hardly would emphasize this for American students as much as the author of Exodus did for his readers.

This consideration of the historical background is important especially when we come to the other lists of sins in the New Testament, particularly in the epistles of St. Paul. Concern for cataloguing sins or vices arose out of a definite situation. The earliest Christians were under the distinct impression that Jesus would return soon in His second and glorious coming. A conviction of this kind obviously was not conducive either to preserving many records or to listing sins to be avoided. In fact, it was just this kind of mentality that could have encouraged, and apparently did encourage, a *laissez-faire* attitude among some Christians. Paul had to face this situation in the Thessalonian community especially, where a strong sense of the Lord's second coming prevailed. And it was precisely because of this situation that the apostle reacted as he did, reminding his converts that ethical behavior was still a requirement for Christians. We can see how lists of sins would be a concern when the Gospel message shifted from an almost exclusive gaze to the future and the second coming of Christ to a consideration of on-going history and the need to address the contemporary culture.

It has been claimed often that Christianity is not a new moral code but a new life in Christ. But this is an oversimplification that could lead to moral laxity, as it apparently did in the Corinthian community. Paul had to write some rather strong words to them concerning their moral conduct: "Can you not realize that the unholy will not fall heir to the kingdom of God? Do not deceive yourselves: no fornicators, idolaters, or adulterers, no sodomites, thieves, misers, or drunkards, no slanderers or robbers will inherit God's kingdom" (1 Corinthians 6:9-10). The sins listed, especially the sexual perversions, were common enough in the Greek cities. The Corinthians, in practicing them, probably had interpreted Paul's message of Christian liberty in the sense of antinomianism, or disregard for all law. But Paul can speak in the same breath of liberty from law and of the moral requirements that flow from living in the Spirit. He writes to the Galatians: "If you are guided by the Spirit, you are not under the law. It is obvious what proceeds from the flesh: lewd conduct, impurity, licentiousness, idolatry, sorcery, hostilities, bickering, jealousy, outbursts of rage, selfish rivalries, dissensions, factions, envy, drunkenness, orgies, and the like. I warn you, as I have warned you before: those who do such things will not inherit the kingdom of God!" (5:18-21). This catalogue, probably derived from the primitive Church teaching, is followed immediately by a catalogue of virtues. They give adequate testimony to the fact that early Christian catechesis did contain specific moral directives and did list specific actions as objectively sinful.

It has been shown, moreover, that a large number of the moral directives in Paul's letters are parallel to statements of Jesus in the Synoptic Gospels. In fact, the apostle makes it a special point at times to indicate Jesus as the source of his command or recommendation: "To those now married, however, I give this command (though it is not mine; it is the Lord's): a wife must not separate from her husband" (1 Corinthians 7:10). This is significant as it shows that Jesus was looked on as a teacher and not solely as exalted Lord and Savior. The catechesis of the early Church was not a total creation but a development of what Jesus has said.

What we have tried to show in the discussion of these lists of vices and virtues is that a catechesis of sin, specifying certain actions as morally reprehensible, is a necessary aspect of the presentation of Christianity. It is true that Paul and the others often depended on Greek and Jewish sources for their catalogues, but they obviously saw them as just as important for Christians as for others. Because of the borrowed nature of most of the lists, we can conclude that the Christians to whom they were presented were not guilty of all the crimes noted. But there must have been a special situation in each of the various communities that evoked the list in the first place.

There is still a distinctive character in Christian morality that a consideration of lists of sins should not allow us to overlook. The Mosaic Law at the time of Jesus contained some 613 precepts that were thought to provide a complete moral code. New Testament Christianity never produced such a code, nor was it thought that any of the lists of sins or of virtues in this sense was complete. And what is more important, the basic law of love was what characterized Jesus' summing up of the Law, as we have seen. Paul, too, in his more general remarks on Christian living, stresses the positive actions, always motivated by love: "Owe no debt to anyone except the debt that binds us to love one another. He who loves his neighbor has fulfilled the law. The commandments, 'You shall not commit adultery; you shall not murder; you shall not steal; you shall not covet,' and any other commandment there may be are all summed up in this, 'You shall love your neighbor as yourself.' Love never wrongs the neighbor, hence love is the fulfillment of the law" (Romans 13: 8-10). We can translate this view into our catechesis of sin by saying that all sins of commission can be summed up in the one great sin of omission, failure to love.

Degrees of Sin

We noted in the beginning those factors that have helped to inculcate a legalistic attitude toward sin. One was the excessive manner in which the distinction was made between mortal and venial sin. It must be stated, first, that the ennui produced by the distinction is not in the distinction itself but in the concern to list exhaustively those actions that are either mortally or venially sinful. Modern moral theologians stress more the basic attitudes that motivate man in his daily living. These are called *fundamental options,* and they refer to those underlying attitudes towards God and man that affect moral decisions. Thus, if man has chosen to direct his whole life completely to self, without regard for God or others, then his state of life can be said to be that of "mortal" sin. All his actions will be affected by this choice. If his basic choice is for God and others, then his wrong actions will be judged as morally venial or serious to the extent that they fail to be in accord with the basic choice.

These modern terms are not found as such in the Bible. But present in the Scriptures is an awareness of degrees of sin. We find there especially the recognition that the Christian is capable of rejecting that fundamental choice of God that his conversion involved. We already have noted that Paul lists those sins that can exclude one from the kingdom of God (1 Corinthians 6:9-10; Galatians 5:19-21). The same kind of basic moral perversion seems to be indicated in the letter to Titus in which the author writes: "Warn a heretic once and then a second time; after that, have nothing to do with him. You must recognize such a person as perverted and sinful; he stands self-condemned" (3 10-11).

One text in the New Testament especially is strong in its statement about the apostate; it illustrates the kind of "mortal" sin of which we are speaking. The author is describing a Christian who had made his basic choice for God and Christ in his original *metanoia*, or total rejection of one's past life and conversion to God, and then falls away from this choice. "For when men have once been enlightened and have tasted the heavenly gift and become sharers in the Holy Spirit, when they have tasted the good word of God and the powers of the age to come, and then have fallen away, it is impossible to make them repent again, since they are crucifying the Son of God for themselves and holding him up to contempt" (Hebrews 6:4-6). It has been remarked that the author is so keenly aware of the salvation won by Christ and of the interior dispositions that lead the Christian to apostasy that he can see no possibility, on the human level, of repentance. But it is unlikely that he would exclude altogether the possibility of God's initiative in leading the sinner back to Himself. There is little doubt, at any rate, that he has in mind here what we would call a "mortal" sin.

Paul also speaks of "the slavery of sin, which leads to death" (Romans 6:16), a statement that implies a moral attitude leading to complete rejection of God and Christ. Then there is the famous saying of Jesus about the blasphemy against the Holy Spirit that will never be forgiven (Mark 3:28-30; Matthew 12:31-32; Luke 12:10). The passage has caused difficulty because of the saving power of God who cannot be limited in His divine initiative. The text, however, does not say that the sin *cannot* be forgiven, but that it *will* not be forgiven. Granted the condition of the man who commits such a blasphemy, he has placed himself in such a situation that he is no longer open to that very power of the Spirit that is able to save him. Certainly involved here is what modern moralists would call a "mortal" sin.

The clearest reference to degrees of sin is found in the first letter of John. In a concluding summary of the letter, where he speaks of the efficacy of prayer, the author writes: "Anyone who sees his brother sinning, if the sin is not deadly, should petition God, and thus life will be given to the sinner. This is only for those whose sin is not deadly. There is such a thing as a deadly sin; I do not say that one should pray about that. True, all wrongdoing is sin, but not all sin is deadly" (5:16-17). It is interesting that we have here the recommendation of prayer for sinners in order that they might be forgiven by God. But the author explicitly excludes from this recommendation "a deadly sin." John does not tell us what he means by a "deadly sin," nor does he give any particular example, if he had one in mind. Quite possibly he had in mind what is implied in the "unforgiven sin" against the Holy Spirit, namely an attitude on the part of the sinner that makes him impervious to the power of prayer. At any rate, the author very clearly indicates a distinction in the gravity of sins, a distinction that modern moralists have tried to clarify with greater precision.

If the biblical authors found it necessary to make distinctions between the degrees of sins, it is no less necessary today. Any catechesis of sin will have to treat this aspect of the subject. But what should be stressed is not, at least primarily or exclusively, the designation of specific sins as mortal or venial. Certainly it should be indicated that certain sinful actions, by their nature, are conducive to an attitude of absolute selfishness. And it is the possibility of such a result that should be brought home to the student, the possibility of "a break with the vital orientation to salvation, a gambling away of the life of grace" (P. Schoonenberg).

Acts of Sin, State of Sin

An analysis of the New Testament reveals that Jesus and the earliest Church spoke more frequently of individual acts of sin, while the later Church developed the idea of a state of sin. Thus, in the Gospels of Matthew, Mark and Luke, the commonly used New Testament word for "sin" invariably refers to specific acts. But as the recognition of the power of sin grew in the Church, and as the Christians reflected on sin in the light of the salvation won by Jesus Christ, they tended to stress more the evil state in which man can live. There is a parallel here with the fundamental option of which we spoke above.

We can note in this development the unwillingness of the New Testament writers to think of morality in too juridical or legalistic a way. Sin as a state of life in which man lives will not be confused too readily with the transgression of a precept—although the state of sin obviously can result from repeated acts of this kind. The point is that the fundamental attitude of man is being emphasized rather than the individual action whose motivation can be difficult at times to recognize and whose real evil or goodness therefore can not always be determined.

Jesus Himself prepared the way for this development by His attitude towards those who were considered to be transgressors of the Law. The scene in Levi's house reveals this attitude towards "offenders against the law." "While Jesus was reclining to eat in Levi's house, many tax collectors and those known as sinners joined him and his disciples at dinner. The number of those who followed him was large. When the scribes who belonged to the Pharisee party saw that he was eating with tax collectors and offenders against the law, they complained to his disciples, 'Why does he eat with such as these?' Overhearing the remark, Jesus said to them, 'People who are healthy do not need a doctor; sick people do. I have come to call sinners, not the self-righteous'" (Mark 2:15-17).

The story seems to have two interpretations, both of which are helpful to our discussion. In the original scene, the sinners clearly were those who were ostracized by the contemporary community by reason of their failure to keep all the precepts of the Law. Jesus associated with them because He knew that, despite their sins, there was an openness in them to His healing love; they did not have the "self-righteousness" of those scribes who felt they were already saved. The early Christian community would have applied this to every man who is called to the Christian faith. He must first recognize his "state of sin" before God if he is to share in Christ's salvation.

Jesus also showed in His attitude to the Law itself an understanding of sin that was not identified necessarily with the transgression of a precept. This was evident especially in the manner in which He acted at times on the Sabbath. The Sabbath rest was observed strictly by most of the Jews at the time, and many discussions were held concerning those acts that violated the Sabbath. Although Jesus was a Jew and observed the Jewish customs and laws, He recognized that these laws were at the service of man, and whenever the dignity of the human person was at stake, He did not hesitate to violate the letter of the Law.

These attitudes manifested to the early Christians something much more profound in the matter of sin than just a violation of a law. This is apparent in the Greek words the biblical authors used at times to translate the sayings of Jesus. In one saying, recorded by Matthew, Jesus states that, on the day of judgment, the "evildoers" will be cast out of His sight (7:23). The Greek word literally means "workers of iniquity," and "iniquity" signifies a state of hostility to God. The real sinners, therefore, are those who are opposed to God's kingdom and whose actions are determined by that underlying opposition.

St. John especially has developed this inner reality of sin as a state or way of life. Only a couple of times in his Gospel does he use the word in the sense of sinful acts. Much more often he uses "sin" in the singular as a designation for sin in general. The most noted use of the word in this sense is the scene where John the Baptist exclaims on seeing Jesus, "Look! There is the Lamb of God who takes away the sin of the world!" (John 1:29). Sin is understood here in the most general way possible, and it is stated that Jesus will gain ultimate victory over the power of sin.

But sin as a state of life also is emphasized by John in a number of other passages. One of the most forceful of these is found in the discourse at the Last Supper where Jesus says, "To hate me is to hate my Father. Had I not performed such works among them as no one has ever done before, they would not be guilty of sin; but as it is, they have seen, and they go on hating me and my Father" (John 15:23-24). The radical nature of sin is brought out by identifying it as a continuing hatred of Christ and the Father.

The same state of existence is shown in John's use of such antitheses as life and death and light and darkness. Sin, for example, is equated with death, obviously a permanent condition, even though man continues to live in his biological condition. "That we have passed from death to life we know because we love the brothers. The man who does not love is among the living dead" (1 John 3:14). Or again, "The judgment of condemnation is this: the light came into the world, but men loved darkness rather than light because their deeds were wicked. Everyone who practices evil hates the light; he does not come near it for fear his deeds will be exposed" (John 3:19-20).

The New Testament, therefore, developed a catechesis of sin far beyond the mere listing of sinful actions. We have seen in our discussion of sin and objective actions that such lists were proposed at times to meet a particular situation in which sinful actions were being practiced by the Christian community. But when the Church reflected on the deeper meaning of Jesus Christ and His saving act of love, she gained a much more profound understanding of the true nature of sin and of man as a sinner.

Sin as Power

This true nature of sin is revealed also in its presentation as a force or power in the world. St. Paul develops this idea especially in his letter to the Romans. He wants to emphasize the saving power of Christ's death and resurrection and what these have done for man. But he recognizes that it is impossible to acknowledge what Christ has done without an adequate acknowledgment of what sin has done. He therefore personifies sin as a power that "reigns" or "rules" over man. And the reign of sin is equated with the reign of death itself. ". . . as sin reigned through death, grace may reign by way of justice leading to eternal life, through Jesus Christ our Lord" (Romans 5:21).

The universality of sin's reign is evident from the fact that it began to exercise its influence from the time of the very first man (Romans 5:12). The actual transgression of Adam is the outward manifestation of sin's rule. And the actual transgressions of all men who followed him are similar manifestations. In other words, Paul distinguishes in these chapters between the actual sins of individual men and the personified power of sin. This development is necessary to show the unique saving power of Christ's actions. To stress that uniqueness, Paul says that not even the Law given by God to Moses on Mount Sinai was able to diminish the power of sin. In fact, he states, "The law came in order to increase offenses . . ." (Romans 5:20). This statement must be understood in context. Elsewhere he says that the law is "holy and the commandment is holy and just and good" (Romans 7:12). Thus, it was not the Law as Law that increased sin. Rather, it brought to man a recognition of sin that he did not have before.

In this discussion of the Pauline catechesis of sin, it can be asked whether the apostle came to an awareness of the power of sin through reflection on the saving power of Jesus Christ or whether reflection on the former gave him his profound appreciation of the latter. The question is legitimate inasmuch as modern catechists might ask whether to emphasize the positive aspect of what Christ brought us, namely life, or the negative aspect of what Christ saved us from, namely sin and death. Some theologians so stress the first seven chapters of the letter to the Romans that they continually present man as a sinner, while others so stress the following chapters of Romans (where the more positive aspect is developed) that for them man is the one redeemed in Christ. The first might more fittingly exclaim, "We are sinners, and *Miserere* is our song." The observation of the latter might be, "We are a paschal people, and *Alleluia* is our song."

But this opposition would be introducing a dichotomy into the New Testament catechesis of sin that really is not there. Paul is very much aware of the tension between these two aspects of man, and in the consideration of any one aspect, he never forgets the other completely. Thus, after telling the Roman Christians that their "old self was crucified with him" (Jesus Christ) and that "his death was death to sin, once for all," he immediately adds, "Do not, therefore, let sin rule over your mortal body . . ." (Romans 6:6-12). In any treatment of the Christian faith, therefore, both man's redemption to life and the existence of sin as power must be presented equally. Reflection on the one should serve to increase the appreciation of the power of the other.

Modern man frequently finds it difficult to recognize sin as a power in the world. Its acknowledgment seems to deny the goodness of God's creation. There is no doubt that the biblical conviction is that God created everything good (cf. Genesis 1). And sin is not viewed as some independent power existing in the world to bring about evil in creation. Rather, it was man himself who introduced this power into the world through his transgression: ". . . through one man sin entered the world and with sin death . . ." (Romans 5:12). This power of man's sin is such that even material creation has been affected. Only *after* Adam's sin does God say to him, "Cursed be the ground because of you! In toil shall you eat its yield all the days of your life" (Genesis 3:17).

Paul makes a similar observation, but he goes on to say that this same material world will share in the redemption won by Christ: "Indeed, the whole created world eagerly awaits the revelation of the sons of God. Creation was made subject to futility, not of its own accord but by him who once subjected it; yet not without hope, because the world itself will be freed from its slavery to corruption and share in the glorious freedom of the children of God" (Romans 8:19-21). In this remarkable statement we can see, first of all, the true power of sin that is able to exercise such influence over created reality. Even modern man, who wants to stress the goodness of things, must recognize here an explanation not only for the evils of war and poverty and racism but also for the ecological imbalances that increasingly plague him.

But we also can see in the statement the profound hope of the apostle. He is the first of the New Testament writers to speak so explicitly of the redemption of the material universe. "For Paul, the created physical universe is not to be a mere spectator of man's triumphant glory and freedom, but is to share in it. When the children of God are finally revealed in glory, death will have no more dominion over them, and the material world will also be emancipated from this 'last enemy' (1 Corinthians 15:23-28). What Paul teaches here will be developed in the Captivity Letters in his notion of the recapitulation of all things in Christ" (J. Fitzmyer). Without a sense of the power of sin, it would have been impossible for him to have understood the full extent of Christ's redemption.

Punishment of Sin

Contemporary moral theology places no stress on the ideas of reward and punishment. The ultimate outcome of one's life is viewed rather as the final expression of that life itself. Eternal reward or punishment is really the transcendent fulfillment of the basic option that one makes. And this view is in accord with the biblical conviction, as will be seen. But since the Bible considers life in all its forms as fundamentally a gift of God—including its transcendent expression— it does speak of reward and punishment. Because of this consideration and because of the traditional usage of the terms, we do speak here of punishment of sin. But it is well to remember that punishment is not to be considered as some imposition from without by an avenging deity.

In the Bible, sin inexorably has its consequences. And just as sin is seen, basically, as a rejection of or offense against God, so is the punishment of sin seen as a retribution sent by God or willed by Him in some way. But there is a very clear development in the biblical understanding of this punishment.

Throughout a good part of the Old Testament period, it was thought that sickness, a short life or a material reverse of any kind was the effect of sin visited on man by God. In the commandment to honor parents, this conviction is reflected indirectly: "Honor your father and your mother, that you may have a long life in the land which the Lord, your God, is giving you" (Exodus 20:12). It is asserted more directly in many of the proverbs: "A kindly man benefits himself, but a merciless man harms himself. The wicked man makes empty profits, but he who sows virtue has a sure reward. Virtue directs toward life, but he who pursues evil does so to his death" (Proverbs 11:17-19). In all of these cases, the consequences both of virtue and of sin are understood as realized in the present life, since there was no firm conviction of an afterlife until late in the Old Testament period.

The association of God in this recompense for good and evil is brought out clearly by the editor of the historical books of Joshua, Judges, 1 and 2 Samuel and 1 and 2 Kings. The writer is presenting a history of the people from the time of the conquest of the land to the exile in Babylon. He sees all the reverses as the punishment of sin and the successes as reward for turning back to God. The exile itself is the ultimate punishment for the sins of the people.

In the second chapter of the book of Judges, the author offers a kind of summary of his theology. There are four parts to it: sin, punishment, repentance, salvation. The people fall away from God, worshipping false idols: "Abandoning the Lord, the God of their fathers . . . they followed the other gods of the various nations around them, and by their worship of these gods provoked the Lord" (Judges 2:12). There immediately follows the punishment sent by God: "Because they had thus abandoned him and served Baal and the Ashtaroth, the anger of the Lord flared up against Israel, and he delivered them over to plunderers who despoiled them" (2:13-14). The repentance of the people and their redemption by God are summed up in this statement: "Whenever the Lord raised up judges for them, he would be with the judge and save them from the power of their enemies as long as the judge lived; it was thus the Lord took pity on their distressful cries of affliction under their oppressors" (2:18).

The biblical author has oversimplified the very complex problem of sin and punishment by identifying military defeat as an expression of God's anger, which is the divine reaction to sin, and by otherwise interpreting the events of history in too simplistic a fashion. Nevertheless, he has pinpointed four of the major factors that continue to form a biblical theology of sin. A contemporary catechesis of sin still would affirm that, once sin is committed, there is punishment for it in some manner, there is always the possibility of repentance, and, if the repentance is true, there is inevitably deliverance from, or forgiveness of, sin. Moreover, that same catechesis would associate God with the process, although it would be much more aware of the mysteriousness of His action.

The punishment of sin by God in the Bible is presented as an expression of His judgment or, even more frequently, of His anger or wrath. While these are necessarily human ways of expressing divine attributes, the reality behind them plays an important part in understanding the idea of punishment of sin. Terms like "anger" and "wrath" are the more human ways of describing God's reaction to sin, but they should not be passed off as mere anthropopathisms (attribution of human passion to God). They expose a belief in a very personal God, in One who reacts vigorously to the actions of man and, in particular, One who fundamentally is opposed to sin. In some few passages in the Old Testament, there is no apparent motive given for the manifestation of God's anger. But in the vast majority of cases, it is quite clear that God's moral will has been offended by sin, and this results in His anger.

References in the New Testament to God's anger are not as frequent as in the Old, a fact that would seem to confirm the false conception that the God of the Old Testament is a God of anger and wrath while the God of the New Testament is one of love. Not only could it be shown that love is an essential component of the relationship between God and Israel, but also it must be stated that God's anger is a part of New Testament theology. Thus, God's anger is referred to in the parables of the merciless official (cf. Matthew 18:34) and of the wedding banquet (Matthew 22:7). And in the other writings, there are a number of references to it. While, as we shall see, the divine reaction to sin is seen in a developed way in the New Testament, to deny the underlying reality of divine anger in the Christian religion would be to remove one of its most basic characteristics.

An even deeper appreciation of punishment of sin perhaps can be had in the notion of God's judgment, which throughout the Bible frequently is used to describe the divine retribution of sin. Although the English word, outside biblical usage, does not mean condemnation of itself, it does give us an insight into the reality under discussion. Judgment represents an attempt to satisfy justice, to bring about a balance in a situation, to restore the right. This at least is the implied conviction behind the biblical use of judgment to describe God's punishment of sin. This is illustrated in the story of Genesis where Abraham is pictured as arguing with the Lord over the fate of the people of Sodom. The patriarch pleads for the safety of all if a number of just men are found in the city. The argument is: "Should not the judge of all the world act with justice?" (Genesis 18:25). In other words, it is a presupposition of the biblical author that any condemnation or punishment of sin by God will be a medium for satisfying justice and establishing the right.

It might seem difficult for some Christians to conceive of the God of love as one who passes adverse judgment on anyone, even a sinner. But the New Testament references to God's judgment, in the sense of condemnation, are sufficient to establish it as a part of the Christian catechesis of sin, even though it is given a fresh interpretation. Besides the Synoptic reference

to the "day of judgment," which is made in the context
of punishment of sin, St. Paul several times uses the
word "judgment" in the sense of divine condemnation.
"We know that God's judgment on men who do such
things is just. Do you suppose, then, that you will escape his judgment, you who condemn these things
in others yet do them yourself?" (Romans 2:3-4).
There is no doubt about the condemnatory sense of
"judgment" here. In some passages, the word "judgment" is even translated "condemnation" in the modern
versions, since that is what is meant. Thus, in Romans
13:2 we read: "As a consequence, the man who op-
poses authority rebels against the authority of God;
those who resist thus shall draw condemnation (or
"judgment") down upon themselves." Finally, Paul
warns the Corinthians of the consequences of their
abuse of the Eucharist: "He who eats and drinks without recognizing the body eats and drinks a judgment
(or "condemnation") on himself" (1 Corinthians
11:29).

With John, we have the most developed concept of
this condemnatory judgment, one that is closest to the
modern interpretation. On the surface, there is an occa-
sional apparent contradiction in the Evangelist's statements about judgment. Thus, Jesus says, "The Father
himself judges no one, but has assigned all judgment
to the Son . . ." (John 5:22). On the other hand, with
seemingly greater insistence, Jesus states, "If anyone
hears my words and does not keep them, I am not the
one to condemn (or "judge") him, for I did not come
to condemn the world but to save it" (John 12:47).

The solution to the paradox is that Jesus does bring judgment inasmuch as His words and works are so radical that they actually do cause man either to accept or reject them. And the rejection leads to condemnation. But the ultimate purpose of Jesus' coming was to save the world from condemnation; as we would say, He does not have a positive will to condemn, but only a permissive will. In other words, it is man himself who actually judges or condemns himself by his rejection of Christ and God. The punishment of sin through judgment, then, is not to be seen as an imposition from without by a capricious judge, but as the inevitable result of sin itself.

Although Paul does not use the word "judgment" in this passage, he speaks of the sins of man as having their "end" in death (Romans 6:21). For Paul, death means more than just biological death. It means complete separation from the source of life: God. And the Greek word for "end" here means more than simply a terminal point. It means the fruition or final expression of what has gone before. Thus, judgment is made by man himself in the very act of sinning.

This concept of self-condemnation is clarified still further by St. John. He sees this condemnatory judgment as taking place in the present, at the very moment of rejection of Christ and the Father. "Whoever believes in him avoids condemnation (literally "is not judged"), but whoever does not believe is already condemned (or "judged") for not believing in the name of God's only Son. The judgment of condemnation is this: the light came into the world, but men loved darkness rather than light because their deeds were wicked" (John 3:18-19). If judgment basically is an act of man himself—or better, the inexorable effect of his sin— then it must occur at the very moment of the sin. And this is what John is saying.

Traditional Christian teaching always has insisted on the "Last Judgment," at which the Father or Christ Himself will pass judgment on all men. Is this excluded by the anticipated judgment of which John speaks? As a matter of fact, John refers to the "Last Judgment" when he writes, "whoever rejects me and does not accept my words already has his judge, namely, the word I have spoken—it is that which will condemn (or "judge") him on the last day" (John 12:48). But there is no contradiction here. The judgment of the "last day" is the confirmation of a judgment already made. As John puts it, he ". . . already has his judge . . ."

We can see, just in this concept of judgment, some of the development in the understanding of punishment of which we spoke at the beginning. But there was another development before this, one that is basic to Christian theology. That is the doctrine of the afterlife. Throughout most of Israel's history, it was thought that at death man entered the shadowy world of Sheol where there was no true life. "Anything you can turn your hand to, do with what power you have; for there will be no work, nor reason, nor knowledge, nor wisdom in the nether world where you are going" (Ecclesiastes 9:10). Obviously, in this mentality, there could be no thought of reward or punishment beyond the grave. That is why the punishment of sin was thought to take place in this life.

But this view brought problems. If sickness, a short life or a reverse of any kind is the result of sin, how is it that a wicked man may prosper and a just man suffer? This problem exercised the minds of some of Israel's greatest writers, among them the author of the book of Job. The theme of the book is precisely the dilemma of a just man who has not sinned, at least not in proportion to the suffering he must bear. After some forty-two chapters, the author has no final solution; the problem of suffering is engulfed in the greater mystery of God Himself. But it can be noted that he does not deny the doctrine of punishment of sin; that is inescapable.

Early in the second century before Christ, we find the first clear reference to the resurrection of the just to everlasting life: "Many of those who sleep in the dust of the earth shall awake; some shall live forever, others shall be an everlasting horror and disgrace" (Daniel 12:2). Similarly, in the story of the Maccabean mother and her seven sons who are put to death by the pagan king, we find several expressions of a belief in bodily resurrection. Thus, the second brother, at the point of death, says, ". . . the King of the world will raise us up to live again forever" (2 Maccabees 7:9). Finally, the book of Wisdom, written shortly before the time of Christ, while it does not explicitly mention bodily resurrection, clearly affirms the reality of eternal life: "But the souls of the just are in the hand of God, and no torment shall touch them" (Wisdom 3:1). "But the just live forever, and in the Lord is their recompense" (Wisdom 5:15). In these books, the belief in everlasting life is established firmly.

The idea of eternal punishment of the wicked is not as clearly developed as is eternal life for the just, but it is referred to, for example, in the passage from Daniel quoted above. This notion, however, was developed in later literature, both inspired and non-inspired. Jesus clearly accepts the notion as is evident from His references to Gehenna, the place of punishment of the wicked (cf. Matthew 5:29-30; 10:28). Gehenna was the name of a valley near Jerusalem where rubbish continually was burned; the fires of Gehenna became symbolic of the eternal torment of sinners. Also, the story of Lazarus contains an illustration of the eternity of punishment. When the rich man asks Abraham for some relief from his torture, the patriarch replies, "Between you and us there is fixed a great abyss, so that those who might wish to cross from here to you cannot do so, nor can anyone cross from your side to us" (Luke 16:26). Finally, mention can be made of that dramatic scene of the last judgment in which the just and the wicked appear before the throne of the Son of Man. To the wicked are addressed these words: "Out of my sight, you condemned, into that everlasting fire prepared for the devil and his angels" (Matthew 25:41).

In the development of the understanding of punishment for sin, therefore, there is a decided shift from a this-worldly to an other-worldly or transcendent concept. This shift was brought on in part, as we saw, by the realization that suffering in this world is not recognizably proportionate to the evil done by man. This was brought home with special force in the case of the wicked prospering and the just suffering unduly. But this shift of understanding does not negate the underlying conviction that, in divine justice, sin cannot go unpunished.

What is the nature of this other-worldly punishment? The idea of torment of some kind runs through most of the texts that speak of it. But the nature of the torment is colored by an imagery evoked by comparisons made with natural or historical phenomena. Thus, the fires in the valley of Gehenna became part of the imagery used to describe the eschatological or other-worldly condition. What happened to Sodom and Gomorrah in the story of Genesis 19 also contributed to the imagery: "He blanketed the cities of Sodom and Gomorrah in ashes and condemned them to destruction, thereby showing what would happen in the future to the godless" (2 Peter 2:6). Christianity has continued to make use of this imagery and even to develop it in its preaching of the Gospel through the centuries.

The imagery may be only that and not intended as a definitive description of eschatological punishment. What is definitive can be learned from a careful analysis of the texts and by comparison with the destiny of the just. In the latter case, it is clear that eternal happiness means, above all, perfect union with God and with the community of the redeemed. If that is its essence, then, by analogy, it would seem that eschatological punishment would consist essentially in separa-

tion from God and from the "sons of God." A study of
the texts that speak of punishment of the damned
confirms this. We can recall the story of Lazarus where
Abraham tells of the eternal chasm "between you (the
condemned rich man) and us." The wicked are similarly addressed in the Matthean story by Christ the
judge: "Out of my sight, you condemned . . ." Literally,
the text reads, "Depart from me . . ." Separation from
God and from the blessed seems to be at the heart of
eschatological punishment for sin.

Is this punishment truly eternal? Certainly the texts
speak of it in this sense. We read of the "unquenchable
fire" of Gehenna (Mark 9:43), of its "everlasting fire"
(Matthew 25:41), of "eternal punishment" (Matthew
25:46), of "the penalty of eternal ruin apart from the
presence of the Lord" (2 Thessalonians 1:9). It is difficult to escape the conclusion that eternity is as much
associated with punishment as it is with reward. This
view, moreover, is in accord with the nature of the sin
that leads inexorably to eternal separation from God:
the sin that totally rejects God and freely chooses to
find happiness in self. The most profound understanding of human freedom, whereby man can freely choose
or reject God, would seem to demand this possibility of
eternal rejection and separation.

Finally, what can be said of the traditional Catholic
doctrine of Purgatory, in which punishment is had for
those sins that do not involve eternal rejection of God?
The question is clouded, once again, by the imagery
used to describe Purgatory and by so much theological
speculation on its nature throughout history. The doc-

trine, as generally presented in the manuals of the past, certainly is not found in Sacred Scripture. It is, therefore, the result of much development in the life of the Church.

Nevertheless, there are two considerations that can be offered. First, there are a couple of texts in the Bible that provided a basis for the later development. The first text is found in 2 Maccabees (not considered inspired by most Protestant churches), where Judas Maccabeus is said to provide for an expiatory sacrifice in Jerusalem for the dead. "Thus he made atonement for the dead that they might be freed from this sin" (12:46). The passage, then, envisages a state in which the dead exist in some way, yet not completely purified.

The second text is a difficult one in 1 Corinthians. Paul is speaking of the reward or punishment that ministers of the Gospel will have in accord with the manner in which they fulfill the ministry. He says that the work of each will be manifested on the day of Christ's second coming. The minister whose work will not meet the test "will suffer loss. He himself will be saved, but only as one fleeing through fire" (3:15). There are many difficulties in the interpretation of the passage, but no doubt it provided a partial basis for the later development of the doctrine of Purgatory.

The second consideration that can be offered is that behind the doctrine is the quite biblical conviction that sin does have its result in punishment. Exactly how the biblical conviction can be made to square with the doctrine of Purgatory is the work of the theologian and of the whole Church.

If we have treated the punishment of sin at some length, it is because it is a consistent teaching of the Scriptures throughout the entire period of biblical revelation. While much of its imagery can be demythologized, the reality still must be affirmed. Second, in the very legitimate desire today to emphasize the positive motive of love rather than the negative motive of fear, there can be the temptation to deny altogether what was proposed as the object of fear, namely, the punishment of sin. If we see that punishment, however, not primarily as the object of fear but as the final expression of irresponsible action, then true Christian freedom *with* responsibility for our choices will be championed more effectively.

Sin and Evil

Man throughout his history has been plagued both by the presence of evil in the world and by the difficulty of explaining it. Commonly accepted is the distinction between physical evil, such as natural calamities—droughts, floods, epidemics—and moral evil—wars, bigotry, crimes—which always is associated with man's free will. The presence of both these kinds of evil hardly needs defending; some of the most profound literature of man was produced out of a recognition of evil's presence and, at times, domination. This presence of evil has forced itself so strongly on some philosophers that they have felt obliged to posit an evil principle to account for it (metaphysical dualism) or an evil world soul (cosmological dualism). This principle or world soul would explain evil in the same way in which God is considered responsible for all that is good.

Such an explanation is totally unacceptable in the framework of ethical monotheism, where the one God is the sole cause of all that is. And, as the priestly author of Genesis put it so clearly, "God looked at everything that he had made, and he found it very good" (1:31). It is this two-fold conviction, namely, that God is the author of all that is and that all He made was good, that produced such a dilemma in the face of evil. One biblical explanation given was an obvious one: evil is the result of man's own sin. In other words, the physical evil man experiences in life is the consequence of the moral evil for which he alone is responsible. This is the explanation offered, for example, by the Yahwist author when he describes the punishment meted out to the man and woman for their sin (cf. Genesis 3:15-19). The punishment includes those physical disabilities that every man experiences in his lifetime. Again, a number of times throughout his work the Deuteronomistic historian (Joshua, Judges, 1 and 2 Samuel, 1 and 2 Kings) mentions that the people or the king suffered reverses because of their sins; physical evil as the divine retribution for moral evil is an essential part of his theology.

Because physical evil was seen as a punishment for sin, it also could be described as coming from God. The anonymous author of the second part of Isaiah was so concerned to stress the absolute uniqueness and monotheistic character of Yahweh that he states without hesitation, "I form the light, and create the darkness, I make well-being and create woe (or "evil"); I, the Lord, do all these things" (Isaiah 45:7). If anything exists, it must come from God. And, clearly, physical evils are a reality. They must come from God, although they have a good end, which is the conversion of man.

Again, we read in Amos: "If evil befalls a city, has not God caused it?" (3:6). Here the concern is to show that any physical evil has its purpose in God's sight and, to this extent, can be said to come from Him. Neither of these writers was concerned with the negative aspect of physical evil, an aspect that would lead later theologians to distinguish between the effective and the permissive will of God. They were concerned, rather, with the ultimate purpose of all reality, including that of physical evil.

Israel was convinced that God saves man from evil. The whole purpose of His redemptive activity in the world is to do away with evil. While the most consistent cry of the prophets is that the people themselves turn away from their evil ways, there is presupposed always the conviction that God is the one who provides the initiative for it. For this reason He is called the "redeemer of Israel" (Isaiah 41:14). It is true that Israel did not make a conscious distinction between physical and moral evil, and, for that reason, it may not be possible always to know which is being referred to in a particular text. But that it is God who is thought ultimately to bring redemption even from physical evil is clear from the oracles concerning the messianic days: "No longer shall the sound of weeping be heard there, or the sound of crying; No longer shall there be in it an infant who lives but a few days, or an old man who does not round out his full lifetime . . ." (Isaiah 65:19-20). This faith-conviction is expressed also in the New Testament (cf. Romans 8:19-21; Revelation 21:1-4).

Thus far, the picture seems fairly clear. Sin is (moral) evil; it constitutes the "evil ways" from which Israel must turn. Sin also is responsible, in some way, for the (physical) evils that plague man. And, inasmuch as they are permitted by God as a punishment of sin, they can be said to come from Him. But God's final purpose in creation is redemption from all evil (both moral and physical).

This rather neat picture had its problems. The one most discussed is that if physical evil is a punishment of sin, there seems at times to be no correspondence between what one man does and the evil he suffers. The book of Job is the classic statement of this case. While it remains part of a greater mystery, as the author of Job concluded (42:1-6), some light is thrown on it by New Testament writers, especially John and Paul. In their treatment of sin as "sin of the world" and as a personified power, we see it as "a powerful virus of evil which has a history of its own on the cosmic plane. The sin of the world is a virus of evil which entered the world as a personified force through original sin and dynamically unfolds itself and tightens its grip on humanity and on the world in an escalating fashion down the ages of history. It is the hidden power which multiplies transgressions in the history of mankind. They are merely its symptoms; it is greater and deeper than all of them. It forms human history into what we might call 'perdition history' " (K. O'Shea). The personal sins of man, in other words, have produced a climate of sin, "the sin of the world," which inevitably affects everyone born into the world.

It is readily apparent how the personal sins of some can bring about physical evils to those who are not guilty of those sins, such as in the cases of wars, poverty caused by social sins, a brutalizing colonialism. Assuredly this introduces the further question of how divine justice is satisfied both in the case of the sinners and in that of the afflicted, although, as we already have seen, the canonical Scriptures propose the doctrine of a transcendent retribution, which is accepted only in faith.

There is a passage in John's Gospel that seems to deny the association of sin with physical evils. When the man born blind was brought to Jesus and the latter was asked whether the man's own sin or his parents' sin had caused this physical evil, Jesus replied, "It was no sin, either of this man or of his parents. Rather, it was to let God's works show forth in him" (9:2-3). But Jesus is not speaking of the cause or origin of the man's blindness; He is speaking of its final purpose, which is the glory of God, manifested in the cure. Blindness is the consequence of sin, but Jesus does not want to discuss its precise origin in the sin of any particular individual. He sees it as one more manifestation of what John calls the "sin of the world." He is more concerned with the ultimate goal of redemptive and perdition history, which is the glory of God.

We can say, then, that in the biblical view moral evil is sin, and physical evil in some way is related always to moral evil, usually as its consequence. In a static world view, where man and nature are related from the very beginning of creation, it is not difficult to see man as responsible through his sin for the physical evils that afflict him, as the punishment meted out to Adam indicates. Just how we would explain that responsibility in the case of such natural calamities as floods may not be clear always, but that biblical man recognized the responsibility is evident from the story of Noah. All of creation was involved in the association. This association with man's sin as well as with his ultimate destiny is expressed beautifully by St. Paul in his letter to the Romans (here as paraphrased by C. F. D. Moule): "For creation with eager expectancy, is waiting for the revealing of the sons of God. For creation was subjected to frustration, not by its own choice, but because of Adam's sin which pulled down nature with it, since God had created Adam to be in close connection with nature" (8:19-20).

Modern man has no difficulty in seeing much of physical evil as the consequence of moral evil. And the modern Christian can believe that God, in His covenant love, will bring to its just fulfillment the whole of creation, both man and nature. In that fulfillment, as Paul assures us, the sufferings of the present are "as nothing compared with the glory to be revealed in us" (Romans 8:18). This is not to be understood as instilling an attitude of resignation to present evils. Quite the contrary; it is precisely because the Scriptures associate these evils with sin that the Christian is encouraged—even commanded—to work towards their overcoming by obedience to the total will of God.

The mystery of evil remains. Whatever may have been its nature in those incredibly long periods of time before the emergence of man on the world scene, as the evolutionary world view depicts it, the mystery of evil has become part of the mystery of sin. Perhaps it would be better to say that those physical calamities and catastrophes were not, before the appearance of man, truly evil; they were the necessary imperfections in the thrust for fulfillment. They remain this even after the appearance of man, but now they take on the nature of evil because their history is associated inextricably with the history of sin. Their ultimate destiny, for the Christian, is revealed in the conquest of evil (the miracles) and of sin (forgiveness) by Jesus Christ, the resurrected Lord.

Original Sin

In any discussion of sin, something should be said about original sin. As a matter of fact, we have alluded to aspects of it in earlier comments, such as when we spoke of sin as a power in the world. But original sin is one of the theological problems of our day, so it demands at least a brief treatment by itself. The problem is not its denial by modern Catholic theologians but its explanation. And it must be noted that the explanation of doctrines of the faith always is subject to further elaboration. As Pope John XXIII stated in his opening address at the Second Vatican Council, "The substance of the ancient doctrine of the deposit of faith is one thing, and the way in which it is presented is another." While the former remains constant, the latter is subject to change. And such a change in presentation or explanation has characterized recent discussion of original sin.

The older explanation was fairly clear and consistent. The first man, Adam, was constituted in a state of perfection, enjoying certain gifts and privileges as a result of his union with God. But he rebelled against God through a personal sin—generally thought to be a sin of pride—and thereby lost his state of innocence and perfection and the accompanying gifts. Moreover, since he was the father of all human beings who came after him, his state of guilt was passed down to all of them. This was not a personal sin on the part of his descendants, but it was a true sin inasmuch as it affected their relationship to God and their possession of the preternatural gifts. When man reached the age of reason, he could affirm, in view of the victory of Christ over sin, his faith in God and thereby achieve salvation. In the Christian dispensation, this was achieved through incorporation into the Body of Christ, the Church, by the sacrament of Baptism. At one time, some theologians thought that infants who died without Baptism, and therefore in the state of original sin, were condemned to hell. The majority of theologians, however, held that they went to Limbo, a place of natural happiness.

Several factors have contributed to a rethinking of this doctrine. On the scientific level, the theory of evolution has presented man not as created in a single moment of time but as evolving gradually from lower forms of life. Thus, in the case of the first "breakthrough" from prehuman to human life, man would have been constituted in a most primitive state, hardly endowed with all the qualities usually associated with the first man in traditional imagery. At some time, of course, he would have been faced with the moral choice between good (acceptance of divine sovereignty, however he may have conceived of it) and evil (seeking only his selfish ends). And the choice of evil would have debilitated him in his relationships with others, whenever the meetings occurred, and with nature itself. But at least the traditional images of Paradise would not be in accord with this reality, unless they are to be interpreted symbolically.

Moreover, if the evolutionary theory is true, it seems more likely that there would have been more than one "breakthrough" from prehuman to human life. This would necessitate the acceptance of polygenism (the descent of the human race from many "first parents") instead of the traditional monogenism (the descent of the human race from a single pair). This view, admittedly, is theory rather than proven scientific fact, but it is a possibility with which the theologian must contend.

On the biblical level, a deeper understanding of the first eleven chapters of Genesis also has conditioned the thinking on original sin, at least in its biblical dimensions. Almost all exegetes—with the exception of the literalists, who interpret every sentence and word according to their literal or surface meaning—agree that the authors of those chapters were not trying to give a precise historical picture of the first days of mankind. They were concerned primarily with man as they knew him in their own time, and they attempted to explain the presence of evil in their own society. Legends and stories of all kinds that came down to them from civilizations more ancient than their own

71

made them aware that evil was present in human society from the beginning; and in their own folk stories of murder, vengeance and natural calamities, they attributed these evils to the personal sin of man. It was their conviction that the God they knew, the God who called and saved His people, could not be responsible for evil. In other words, they were more concerned with depicting the universality of sin and man's ultimate responsibility for it than sin's precise historical origin.

St. Paul also wrote of the sin of the first man and, seemingly, in a way that would agree with the traditional explanation of original sin (even though the phrase "original sin" never occurs in the Bible). In Romans 5:12-19, he speaks of sin and death entering the world through one man, of a single offense bringing condemnation to all men, and of all men becoming sinners through one man's disobedience. The precise meaning of the whole passage has been debated heatedly over the centuries, and it is impossible here to go into any details on the debate. But it can be stated with certainty that Paul establishes a causal connection between the first sin and death and between the first sin and the sins of all mankind. And this, it seems, is at the heart of the Catholic teaching on original sin. It is the more precise understanding of these connections that modern theologians are debating.

First, death is understood by St. Paul not in the merely biological sense but in the total sense of complete estrangement from the source of life who is God. This, of course, would include the eventual cessation of physical life, but it would be distorting Paul's theology to think of it solely, or even primarily, in this sense. For the apostle, death, like sin, is personified and depicted as a cosmic force in the world, the last enemy to be overcome by the victory of Jesus Christ (1 Corinthians 15:54-57). Since death is seen as such a total estrangement from God, it is understandable that there should be a most intimate connection between death and sin. Sin, as should be clear from all we have said about it, is fully responsible for the introduction of death. And the sin of the first man would have first introduced death, in this wider sense, into the world. The causal connection between sin and death, then, is evident.

The connection between the sin of the first man and the condition of all other men is more complex. In the older theology, it was taught that original sin was passed on down "by generation," that is, through the marriage act whereby the child is conceived. The explanation can be understood properly enough, although it is a bit simplistic, emphasizing perhaps too much the concept of original sin as a "stain" on the soul or as some kind of spiritual deformity that is inherited. Yet it is at the heart of the Pauline teaching as well as of Catholic doctrine that "through one man's disobedience all became sinners . . ." (Romans 5:19).

With the emphasis on the biblical notion of sin as an evil force or power *in the world*, theologians today speak more readily of the child being conceived in the "situation" of sin, whereby his ability to act freely for the good is weakened decidedly. This situation was first caused, of course, by the first sin, and since that time,

73

it has affected all men. There is, therefore, a true connection between the first personal sin and the sinful condition of all mankind. Moreover, the personal sins of all men have helped to increase the power of this "sin of the world," although it has been adversely affected, and ultimately is to be overcome, by the elements of salvation sown by Jesus Christ.

Another biblical emphasis made by modern theologians is that of every man's solidarity with all mankind, not in the sense of some magical effect had on another by one's act, but in the sense of a "situation" or "condition" created by that act. If one is part of the world, it is impossible not to be affected by that action, unless there were some special preventive action taken.

A couple of statements of contemporary theologians who have studied the question perhaps will be of help. "In this framework, original sin appears as the weight of evil that burdens every man by his birth and his solidarity with all mankind, prior to all his sins, but ratified and freely accepted by each personal sin. Theology ordinarily describes sin on the analogy of 'habit,' an inclination of the will resulting from personal choices. But original sin can also be depicted as the situation in which man finds himself because he enters a world where sin reigns" (P. Smulders). "We have to speak of the influence which one man's decision has on that of another in such a way that the freedom of the second man is preserved. The notion of situation can be helpful here. My free act puts the other in a situation which presents him with good or evil, provides support or withdraws it, and communicates values and norms" (P. Schoonenberg).

According to these explanations, which admittedly are tentative, the sin of the first man inevitably would have produced a condition or situation of sin in the world and all other men would have been affected by it through birth into this world. A state of personal enmity between the newly conceived child and God would not exist, a point implicitly contained in the teaching that the child is not conceived in *personal* sin. Through Baptism, however, the person, including the infant, is brought into a direct personal relationship with Jesus Christ through His Body, which is the Church. Being brought into this community of redemption, the person plainly is being removed from the situation of evil, from "the sin of the world," and thereby helped to make the morally good personal choices when confronted with them. In other words, through Christ's Body, the Church, and through the sacraments of the Church, God's loving and saving presence is rendered more available to the individual so that the community of salvation gradually is built up and strengthened.

As mentioned, no one would claim that a final, exhaustive explanation of original sin has been attained; it is part of the whole mystery of sin itself and so will never be understood thoroughly. At the same time, it does seem that the contemporary explanations are more compatible with the developments in the scientific understanding of the history of the world and of man and with the developments in the exegesis of the Scriptures. There remains the conviction of faith that there is original sin and that all men are affected by it. Or, to put it in the more optimistic terms of St. Paul, "To sum up, then: just as a single offense brought condemnation to all men, a single righteous act brought all men acquittal and life. Just as through one man's disobedience all became sinners, so through one man's obedience all shall become just" (Romans 5:18-19).

Victory over Sin

The heart of the Christian Gospel is that Jesus came to save us from our sins. The name Jesus itself contains this message; it means literally "Yahweh is salvation." This is stated also in the words of the angel to Joseph, "She is to have a son and you are to name him Jesus because he will save his people from their sins" (Matthew 1:21). Moreover, Jesus' victory over sin was conceived primarily to have been effected through His death on the cross. "I handed on to you first of all what I myself received, that Christ died for our sins in accordance with the Scriptures . . ." (1 Corinthians 15:3). "It is precisely in this that God proves his love for us: that while we were still sinners, Christ died for us" (Romans 5:8). ". . . the blood of his Son Jesus cleanses us from all sin" (1 John 1:7). "In his own body he brought your sins to the cross, so that all of us, dead to sin, could live in accord with God's will. By his wounds you were healed" (1 Peter 2:24).

All of these theological statements can find their basis in the earthly ministry of Jesus. John the Baptist, whose ministry was preparatory to that of Jesus, preached "a baptism of repentance which led to the forgiveness of sins" (Mark 1:4). According to John's Gospel, the Baptist's identification of Jesus was precisely as "the Lamb of God who takes away the sin of the world" (1:29).

Perhaps the most obvious indication of Jesus' awareness that His mission was to overcome sin is the manner in which He associated with sinners and responded to those who reprimanded Him for such association. A familiar theme in all the Gospels is the scandal caused by His keeping company with sinners. St. Luke emphasizes this theme more than the others; one of the titles given his work is the "Gospel of sinners." Luke is the only evangelist to include the story of the sinful woman who anointed Jesus' feet (7:36-50); the parables of the lost sheep, of the lost coin, of the prodigal son (c. 15); Jesus' forgiving words to His executioners (23:34); and His words of assurance to the criminal hanging with Him (23:43). Luke evidently recognized the significance of Jesus' presence with sinners, and he used those stories that illustrated it.

That such a presence was significant is evident from the reaction it aroused in Jesus' contemporaries: "The tax collectors and sinners were all gathering around to hear him, at which the Pharisees and the scribes murmured, 'This man welcomes sinners and eats with them'" (Luke 15:1-2). It is on this occasion that Luke records the three parables mentioned above. These are provocative stories whose purpose is to show the Father's concern for the lost sheep, the lost coin, the prodigal son—in short, for the sinner. That is what the reign of God, which was the central message of Jesus, is all about.

In a more direct way, Jesus speaks of His mission to sinners. Once some scribes noticed that Jesus was eating with tax-collectors and sinners, and they complained to His disciples. "Overhearing the remark, Jesus said to them, 'People who are healthy do not need a doctor; sick people do. I have come to call sinners, not the self-righteous'" (Mark 2:15-17). This is a remarkable statement, and it can be appreciated better if compared with a similar statement attributed to the Teacher of Righteousness, a leader of the Essenes of the famous Dead Sea community. In one of the hymns, he says, "And I have been a snare for sinners, but healing for all those that are converted from sin . . ." (Hymn Scroll, 11, 8-9). According to this statement, the mission of the Teacher was to those who already had been converted.

The most explicit statement in the Synoptic Gospels about the significance of Jesus' death as victory over sin is found in the words of institution of the Eucharist: "Then he took a cup, gave thanks, and gave it to them. 'All of you must drink from it,' he said, 'for this is my blood, the blood of the covenant, to be poured out in behalf of many for the forgiveness of sins'" (Matthew 26:27-28). Jesus' death is compared with a sacrificial death of the Old Testament in which, by the sprinkling of blood on both parties, a covenant was formed. Matthew would have been aware that certain Old Testament sacrifices did atone for *ritual* offenses, but when he adds "for the forgiveness of sins," there is no qualification.

The manner in which Jesus' victory over sin was achieved is described in several ways in the New Testament literature. It would be helpful to consider these individually, if briefly, since this victory is such an integral part of our Christian faith. Certainly no modern catechesis of sin would be complete without a consideration of its defeat by Jesus Christ.

One of the more common expressions of Christ's victory is "salvation," or "save." It is interesting that in the earlier books of the New Testament, Jesus is rarely called "savior," probably because of the fear that some might equate Him with one of the "saviors" in the pagan cults, where the title was fairly common. But there was no hesitation about saying that Jesus "saved." When that word is used in the Synoptic Gospels, it almost always refers to some activity of Jesus whereby someone is healed or kept from harm. But in a number of passages, it is argued that the Evangelists see this physical salvation as a symbol of a greater salvation. If so, it helps us to make more concrete and vivid our conception of salvation and to realize the intimate bond between physical and spiritual salvation.

What the greater salvation is to which the healing narratives point is clear from explicit statements, some of which we have seen. Quite simply, it is salvation from sin. Note how Jesus as savior is connected with the forgiveness of sins in this passage from Acts: "He whom God has exalted at his right hand as ruler and savior is to bring repentance to Israel and forgiveness of sins" (5:31). We have seen enough of these texts to understand that salvation for Christians meant liberation from sin. Seen in this way, salvation is a negative concept; it does not have a positive connotation. If, however, the New Testament doctrine of salvation from sins was developed within the context of Jesus' healing activity, then there is a positive element included. Salvation is not only liberation from sins; it is a making whole. Whatever else the effect of sin is, it is that it destroys wholeness of being and of relationships. Salvation, by destroying sin, restores this wholeness.

A frequently used term to describe the saving work of Jesus, at least by modern theologians, is "redemption." The term actually is used very sparingly in the New Testament; the concept never was developed as much as others were. But it is an interesting term, and it allows us one more insight into Christ's victory over sin.

The English word "redeem" comes from the Latin, meaning literally "to buy back." This is also the meaning of the Greek word. The concept of ransom is inherent in the word. It was used often in Greek society to describe the action whereby a slave was released from captivity upon the payment of a specified sum of money. It would be tempting to see this custom as the only necessary background for an understanding of New Testament redemption by Christ. And some of the texts seem to support this contention. For example,

"The Son of Man has not come to be served but to serve —to give his life in ransom for the many" (Mark 10: 45). The word "ransom" here is connected with another Greek word for "redemption." Or again, "You have been purchased, and at a price" (1 Corinthians 6:20). In these and similar texts, there is included certainly the idea of a ransom being paid, which would be the life of Jesus Christ, as well as the notion of liberation. Although they do not state explicitly what man has been liberated from, there is no doubt that sin was understood. Thus, after Paul states that all men have sinned, he adds, "All men are now undeservedly justified by the gift of God, through the redemption wrought in Christ Jesus" (Romans 3:24). Even more clearly is it stated, "Through him we have redemption, the forgiveness of our sins" (Colossians 1:14).

While the Greek custom of ransoming slaves does contribute something to the understanding of redemption by Christ, it should not be pressed too far. It is more likely that the Old Testament idea of Yahweh ransoming His people from slavery in Egypt (cf. Deuteronomy 7:8) or buying or acquiring them for Himself (cf. Exodus 6:6-7) is behind the New Testament usage. In this way, then, we understand redemption, not only in its negative aspect as liberation from sin, but also in its positive aspect as liberation for Christ. Christians have been acquired by Christ and now belong completely to Him and to the Father. "He is the pledge of our inheritance, the first payment against the full redemption of a people God has made his own, to praise his glory" (Ephesians 1:14).

God, of course, could have forgiven sins without the necessity of a redemption in which such a high price (or ransom) had to be paid. Although it is never possible to understand fully the workings of God's providence, the fact that He did choose the way of redemption underscores the reality of sin. Liberation is not an easy matter because that from which we are liberated is so harsh and powerful. When we reflect on our Christian liberty, then, we will appreciate it all the more when we recognize the reality of sin. "You have been bought at a price!" (1 Corinthians 7:23).

In Romans 3:25, Paul makes use of a special word to express Christ's victory over sin, a word that he only uses in this place but that has become part of the classical vocabulary of the theology of sin. The word is "expiation." "Through his blood, God made him the means of expiation for all who believe. He did so to manifest his own justice, for the sake of remitting sins committed in the past . . ." Again, if we consider only the non-biblical usage of the word "expiate," we will have a false notion of what is meant, but a notion that probably has influenced many Christians. In pagan usage, it usually meant to placate an angry God. This is far from the Pauline sense.

The Old Testament equivalent of the New Testament word usually has God as the subject, not the object. The verb means "to wipe away." Obviously this would be understood as wiping away the sins of man. And this seems to be the sense that Paul intended as the context suggests. Expiation, then, is the wiping away of our sins through the blood of Christ.

But there is more. The Greek word used by Paul in the text of Romans is used in the Greek version of the Old Testament to describe an object in the Holy of Holies in the Jerusalem temple. It may be the lid over the ark of the covenant that symbolized God's presence among His people. On the Day of Atonement (Yom Kippur), the high priest sprinkled blood on this object (translated as "mercy seat" or "propitiatory"), thus atoning for his sins and those of the people. When Paul, therefore, calls Christ this "means of expiation," he well may have had in mind the picture of Christ as the seat of God's mercy on His people.

Paul's emphasis that expiation was achieved through Christ's blood merits some explanation. In the Bible, blood is not a sign of death, and the blood of sacrificed animals was not considered the price paid by man to an angry and demanding God. Rather, blood was the sign of life and, as such, was considered sacred. It was used to dedicate something or someone to Yahweh. The shedding of an animal's blood, therefore, symbolized the dedication of the offerer's life to Yahweh. Paul is saying that, by shedding His blood and so willingly offering His life to God, Christ wiped away the sins of man and made it possible for man to be reconciled or dedicated to God.

An expression that is used by St. Paul, especially in his letters to Galatians and Romans, to describe the victory over sin is "justification." The concept is not emphasized in other New Testament writings, and it is developed by Paul only in these two letters. The development was occasioned by his concern for some Christians who were tempted to think that they had to practice the works of the Mosaic Law if they wanted to be true Christians. Paul's vigorous response is that man is justified by faith and not by law.

The Greek word for "justification" is related closely to another word translated as "righteousness" or "justice." And often this term is associated with God. God's righteousness or justice has a juridical note about it; it suggests a decision made in favor of His people, Israel. It is connected closely with God's covenant love whereby His relationship with His people is established. This is important to keep in mind, since it will obviate a too juridical understanding of what takes place, although this is present.

To put Paul's thesis as simply as possible, through the power of God alone man is justified or placed in a state of righteousness because of his association with the saving events of Jesus Christ. "To sum up, then: just as a single offense brought condemnation to all men, a single righteous act brought all men acquittal (or "justification") and life" (Romans 5:18). Through the translation "acquittal," the juridical nature of the action is emphasized. The question is asked whether Paul sees only a declaratory action on the part of God in justification or whether he intends by the word a true interior change of the man who is justified. The emphasis here seems to be on the declaration by God. But there is sufficient evidence in other passages of Paul to indicate that he thought in terms of a radical change in man. His sins truly are wiped out.

In the concept of justification, then, there is an emphasis on God's power, on a declaration of righteousness of man based on God's own righteousness, on the actions of Jesus Christ that are salvific in and of themselves, and on the appropriation by man of these saving actions through faith. Sin itself is not included directly in the concept of justification, although it should be obvious that the notion would have no meaning without the presupposition of sin. Only he can be made righteous who was unrighteous before.

The final concept that is used to describe Christ's victory over sin in the New Testament is "reconciliation." It appears to be the most positive of all the concepts, and it includes a number of insights that enrich our understanding of what happens in the Christian faith. The term is associated with a Greek word meaning "to change," "to exchange," or "to make peace." While the last meaning is closest to Paul's use, the other meanings are not entirely absent. The earliest reference is in 2 Corinthians 5:18-20. "All this has been done by God, who has reconciled us to himself through Christ and has given us the ministry of reconciliation. I mean that God, in Christ, was reconciling the world to himself, not counting men's transgressions against them, and that he has entrusted the message of reconciliation to us. This makes us ambassadors for Christ, God as it were appealing through us. We implore you, in Christ's name: be reconciled to God!"

That a complete and total change is involved in this reconciliation of man and the world is clear from the preceding verse where Paul speaks of the new creation in Christ, of the old order passing away (v. 17). The active role of God also is stressed, even though two parties are involved. We can note that the initiative is the Father's, not Christ's. God reconciles man through Christ. Though man does not initiate reconciliation, he does not remain completely passive. Rather, he is made active and is entrusted with the "ministry of reconciliation." The idea of a change brought about in man also is included in the passage from Romans: "For if, when we were God's enemies, we were reconciled to him by the death of his Son, it is all the more certain that we who have been reconciled will be saved by his life" (5:10). Here the notion of victory over sin is clear, since those who are reconciled were once "God's enemies," that is, through sin.

While the idea of a cosmic reconciliation already is hinted at in the passage from 1 Corinthians, it is much more developed in Colossians 1:19-20: "It pleased God to make absolute fulness reside in him (Christ) and, by means of him, to reconcile everything in his person, both on earth and in the heavens, making peace through the blood of his cross." The preceding verses had spoken of everything as having been created in Him—that is, Christ—through Him and for Him. Now, since all these things are reconciled with God through Christ, the supposition is that they had been infected by man's sin. Here, too, for the first time, reconciliation explicitly is paralleled with "making peace." The old state of enmity and even of war now has been declared over; a new state of peace is present. In the letter to the Ephesians, Paul calls Christ Himself "our peace" inasmuch as He reconciled both Jew and Gentile to God (2:14-16).

All these texts either presuppose or propose a state of enmity that had existed between man and God. It was an enmity or an alienation that had been introduced by the rebellion of sin. There was a state of at-odds-ment that man simply could not overcome. It was the act of God in Jesus Christ that healed the wound, or bridged the chasm between man and God, and thus brought about a state of at-one-ment, the English word that frequently is used to translate the biblical term of reconciliation.

An appreciation of the reality of sin and of the victory over sin go hand in hand. A realization of the one is affected by a realization of the other. In the early Church, the awareness of what had occurred in the Christ event evoked a certain tension between the "already" and the "not yet." Salvation already had been achieved in the person of Jesus Christ, but that salvation had not yet been effected in the whole of creation. The tension continues to exist until the end of history when the victory of Christ over the power of sin will have been extended to all things. "Just as in Adam all die, so in Christ all will come to life again, but each one in proper order: Christ the first fruits and then, at his coming, all those who belong to him. After that will come the end, when, after having destroyed every sovereignty, authority, and power, he will hand over the kingdom to God the Father" (1 Corinthians 15:22-24).

Conversion from Sin

Man, even now, can share in Christ's victory over sin. The power of Christ's redemption is not held completely in abeyance until the end of time. One of the terms used in the New Testament to express this present participation by man in the victory is "conversion." The Greek word also is translated frequently as "repentance."

The notion of conversion already was developed in the Old Testament, especially by the prophets, although the biblical authors do not seem to have formed a technical word for the concept. The word most frequently used to express what happened is "turn back," and it almost always was used in the verb form. What is implied, of course, is the return to a situation that previously had prevailed, although in its biblical use the emphasis is on "turning" rather than on "returning."

By its nature, conversion or repentance would seem to be something individual and personal, since an entire change of attitude and of resulting action is implied. But the call also is made to Israel as a people, and the community context never would be forgotten, even in the case of individual conversion. Such a call to the people as a whole is found, in one of the most powerful passages on conversion in the Old Testament, in the second chapter of Hosea. Israel is portrayed as a wife who has left her husband and gone after other lovers. The prophet goes on to describe the turning back of Israel and its result. With Jeremiah, we can note a marked emphasis on individual conversion, which is consistent with the interiorization and spiritualization of religion stressed by this prophet. Several times in the course of his ministry, Jeremiah cries out to the people of Judah and Jerusalem: "Return, each of you, from his evil way; reform your ways and your deeds" (18:11; 25:5; 36:3.7).

With the growth in the personal element of conversion, there also is a greater emphasis on the totality of the change that must take place. Again, the prophets especially are responsible for this. They increasingly were aware that the liturgies of repentance, which included such practices as fasting, wearing sackcloth and ashes, public lamentation and confession of sins, were not of themselves sufficient. In fact, they were absolutely useless unless there was a true interior change of mind and heart. That is why the prophets at times speak of the heart as being involved in conversion: "Yes, when you seek me with all your heart, you will find me with you, says the Lord, and I will change your lot . . ." (Jeremiah 29:13-14).

In the concept of conversion, the emphasis rightly

is on turning *to* God. But always the presupposition is that a turning *from* sin also is involved. In other words, the very idea of conversion would be impossible outside the context of sin and personal rebellion against God. Sin has set up the barrier between man and God. A very clear affirmation of this duality is found in the latter part of the book of Isaiah: "Lo, the hand of the Lord is not too short to save, nor his ear too dull to hear. Rather, it is your crimes that separate you from your God. It is your sins that make him hide his face so that he will not hear you" (59:1-2). Conversion involves a renunciation of the sins that caused the separation; without that a return to God is impossible. "Thus says the Lord God: Return and be converted from your idols; turn yourselves away from all your abominations" (Ezekiel 14:6). "He shall come to Zion a redeemer to those of Jacob who turn from sin, says the Lord" (Isaiah 59:20).

We can see that in this theology of conversion the great stress seems to be on man who makes the decision, turns to God and reforms his life. For the Christian, this is the response he makes to what God has effected through Jesus Christ. But an important point here is that it is a response. In biblical religion, it is always God who takes the initiative. This is true also in the case of conversion. As the author of Lamentations put it so clearly, "Lead us back to you, O Lord, that we may be restored . . ." (5:21). That also could be translated, "Convert us that we may be converted." The insistence on the divine initiative was necessary if man was not to drown in a sea of despair. The history of Israel was a record of failures that made it more and more conscious of the need for divine help. This does not at all detract from the effort required by man but gives it greater motivation.

All the elements of conversion in the Old Testament are found in the New Testament doctrine. But now conversion or repentence takes on greater intensity. The gift of grace in Jesus Christ is so overwhelming that man must be more profoundly aware of his sins and turn to God. Thus, the totality of conversion is even more stressed. We already have seen, in our study of the degrees of sin, the passage in Hebrews 6:4-6 that suggests that, once man has made this total conversion to God and then renounces it, it is not possible, from the human standpoint, for him to renew it.

Most of the references to repentance in the New Testament are found in the Gospels and Acts of the Apostles. It is understandable that Jesus would Himself have preached repentance since the reign of God was being manifested in His coming. St. Mark provides this highly charged summary of Jesus' message: "This is the time of fulfillment. The reign of God is at hand! Reform your lives and believe in the Gospel" (1:15). And the effect of Jesus on man, when he recognizes who He is, is the acknowledgment of his sins, the first necessary step in conversion. Thus did Peter cry out, when he recognized the true nature of Jesus in the miraculous catch of fish, "Leave me, Lord. I am a sinful man" (Luke 5:8).

The Acts of the Apostles record the efforts of the earliest missionaries to bring the good news of Jesus

Christ to the world. Again and again we read that, after detailing what God had done through Jesus Christ, they would conclude with the admonition: "Therefore, reform your lives (or "be converted")! Turn to God, that your sins may be wiped away!" (Acts 3:19).

It very well may be that there are few references to conversion in the letters of the New Testament because these were written for Christian communities who presumably already had turned to God and had reformed their lives. But Paul refers to the repentance of the Corinthians when he recalls the distress his first letter to them had caused, a distress that "led to repentance" (2 Corinthians 7:9). And he goes on to say that "Sorrow for God's sake produces a repentance without regrets (which could also be translated "an unrepented repentance"), leading to salvation . . ." (v. 10). Here Paul stresses the totality involved in a sincere conversion.

Conversion from sin to God, then, is the first step in the order of salvation. It is an acknowledgment of the victory that Christ has won over sin, a victory whose effects now are begun to be applied to the individual man. It is a deeply interior act of man that involves a whole change in his manner of living. It can be accompanied by external "signs of repentance," such as were practiced by Israel in the Old Testament period. But these signs are useless unless the heart has been changed and sin has been renounced.

Forgiveness of Sin

We have delayed until now the discussion of the forgiveness of sin. For two reasons. First, for the Christian, sin is forgiven only through Jesus Christ and through His saving acts. Thus we had to treat first of His victory over sin. The second reason is that in the New Testament there is the further question of the Christians' forgiveness of one another. Thus, all that we have said about sin reaches a climax in the notion of forgiveness, both by God and by man.

The removal of sin is a basic concern of religion. In the pagan religions, this was thought to be accomplished by magic rites. For example, the so-called "sin-eater" removed the sins of a dead person by eating food that had been placed on the corpse's chest. In a part of India, a holy man would be called to the bedside of a dying rajah, embrace him and proclaim that he was taking on himself the dying man's sins. Then, with ten thousand rupees as recompense, he would leave the country forever.

There are traces of similar customs found in the Old Testament, although they are changed radically in meaning by Israel's concept of God. On the Day of Atonement, for example, the priest placed his hands on the head of a goat and confessed the sins of the community. The goat then was driven off into the desert, symbolically carrying the sins with him. The rite was intended to symbolize what God had done for Israel, but always there was the danger that the divine action would be forgotten and all the significance attached to the exterior rite itself.

The divine act of forgiveness of sins is emphasized in the Old Testament, an emphasis that distinguishes Israel's religion from that of the pagans. Motives frequently are adduced why Yahweh should forgive sins —for example, because the petitioner is "alone and afflicted" (Psalm 25:16-18). But just as frequently, no motive is mentioned; it simply is taken for granted that He is a forgiving God. In at least one instance, His forgiveness is attributed to His covenant love for Israel (cf. Numbers 14:19)—in other words, to that special relationship established with the people by God Himself. We can say, then, that forgiveness of sins by God is a necessary component of Israel's religious faith.

"It is I, I, who wipe out, for my own sake, your offenses; your sins I remember no more" (Isaiah 43: 25). These words of the prophet make it clear that forgiveness of sins is a gift of God and that, basically, it is not motivated by human considerations. This does not mean, however, that man was not expected to play a role. There is frequent reference in the Old Testament to certain penitential rites associated with forgiveness of sins. The book of Daniel, for example, records a prayer of the prophet in which these acts are associated in some way with sin: "I turned to the Lord God, pleading in earnest prayer, with fasting, sackcloth, and ashes. I prayed to the Lord, my God, and confessed, 'Ah, Lord, great and awesome God, you who keep your merciful covenant toward those who love you and observe your commandments! We have sinned, been wicked and done evil; we have rebelled and departed from your commandments and your laws . . . But yours, O Lord, our God, are compassion and forgiveness . . . When we present our petition before you, we rely not on our just deeds, but on your great mercy. O Lord, hear! O Lord, be attentive and act without delay, for your own sake, O my God, because this city and your people bear your name!" (9:3-5.9.18-19).

Among the penitential acts mentioned in this prayer are fasting, observing external signs of mourning and confession. All of these require some effort on the part of man, and it might be argued that these are understood as the reason why God should forgive sins. And certainly it is a temptation almost inherent in the acts themselves to think that they produce the forgiveness. The temptation has been succumbed to frequently in the history of religions. It is very clear, however, that this is not the understanding of the biblical author. Daniel says explicitly that "we rely not on our just deeds, but on your great mercy." And the Lord is asked to be attentive "for your own sake." Because "yours . . . are compassion and forgiveness," they can come only from Him and are not dependent on man and his actions. Daniel did not think that, in praying and fasting, he was making up for something that was lacking and that was required for divine justice. Forgiveness of sins is the Lord's totally.

What, then, was the purpose of these acts? We can recall that it is a firm conviction of biblical faith that all sin is punished in some way. This punishment at times was identified with a specific plague or military defeat and simplistically associated with specific sins. Still, these "natural" horrors are the effects of sin; that underlying conviction remains valid. Therefore, the apparent diminution of one's being in some way, such as by fasting or the wearing of sackcloth, is an external expression that symbolized the punishment that the sinner knew was the result of his sins. In other words, these acts are ultimately for man's benefit, not for God's. They help to make man more conscious of his sins and of his need for God's forgiveness. And an awareness of that need, an openness to the divine healing grace, is necessary before God can forgive the sins. That is why these penitential acts are at times presented almost as a condition for forgiveness. They are a condition only to the extent that they produce in man a sense of his status before God. And this is the important point: they produce this sense of one's status before God. It they do not do that, then they are mere play-acting, or they are intended to impress others with one's "holiness," or they are looked upon as magic rites that inevitably produce their effect. In all these cases, the prophet would say, "Rend your hearts, not your garments, and return to the Lord, your God" (Joel 2:13). But to the extent that the acts do produce in man this awareness, to that extent are they always valid religious expressions.

Another aspect of this association of penitential acts with the forgiveness of sins concerns the dramatic element in biblical religion. Salvation is presented as a divine-human drama in which the victory over sin is won through a succession of acts of God. Man has an essential part in this drama to the extent that he either responds or fails to respond to the divine initiative. The whole drama is represented in the sacrifices and other ritual actions of the Old Testament and in the Eucharist and other sacraments of the New Testament. In this context of the drama, penitential acts are seen as having value. They "underline the power and the love of God displayed in his act of deliverance. To put it somewhat bluntly, their penitential practices were intended to make the setting all the more sombre, in order that God's rescue might stand out all the more clearly and convincingly, and thus strengthen their faith and confidence in his love and mercy for them" (T. Worden). Again, it is stressed that the actions are intended for man, for his instruction and motivation, not for God's edification.

In the Old Testament, the priests of Israel had some role in the rites that were used in the forgiveness of certain sins, but they did not express a formula of absolution. This was restricted solely to God. Moreover, even though the forgiveness of sins is connected in a special way with the messianic age (cf. Jeremiah 31:34), it is never stated that the Messiah would forgive sins himself. This introduces us to the New Testament development.

When Jesus declared that the sins of the paralyzed man were forgiven, the reaction of the scribes is understandable in the light of Old Testament teaching; "He commits blasphemy! Who can forgive sins except God alone?" (Mark 2:5-7). But by healing the man's sickness, Jesus intended to vindicate His power to forgive sins. Now, for the first time, the divine power is exercised by one "on earth" (Mark 2:10). Mark quite likely understood this exercise of power "on earth" as extended to the risen Lord now operating through His Church. In other words, we have here an insight into the Church's recognition of the power she had on earth through her identification with the glorified Jesus. This is brought out more clearly in Matthew's version of the story, which differs from Mark's in some important details. At the end of the story, Matthew adds: "At the sight, a feeling of awe came over the crowd, and they praised God for giving such authority to men" (Matthew 9:8). The mention of authority given "to men" suggests that the evangelist is aware of the authority being exercised in the Church of his day. And this is consonant with what Matthew adds later about Jesus telling the community that whatever it declared bound or loosed on earth would be so declared in heaven (18: 18). Finally, John provides us with the scene in the upper room on Easter Sunday when Jesus gave the twelve apostles the power to forgive sins or to hold them bound (20:23).

All of the texts cited are at the basis of the development of the Sacrament of Penance within the Catholic Church. With on-going history, there was a preoccupation with the fact, evidenced already in Paul's epistles, that the Christian who had died to sin through Baptism into the Body of Christ continued to sin. It is not surprising that Christians should conclude, in the light of these sayings of Jesus, that the One who had forgiven sins "on earth" continues to forgive sins "on earth" through the instrumentality of His Church.

Another characteristic of the Christian doctrine on forgiveness is the insistence on the need for mutual forgiveness. If we expect God to forgive us our sins, then we must stand ready to forgive those who have offended us. This injunction is found in a familiar saying of Jesus: "If you bring your gift to the altar and there recall that your brother has anything against you, leave your gift at the altar, go first to be reconciled with your brother, and then come and offer your gift" (Matthew 5:23-24). There is a similar saying in Mark: "When you stand to pray, forgive anyone against whom you have a grievance so that your heavenly Father may in turn forgive you your faults" (11:25). This is the only occurrence of the phrase "heavenly Father" in Mark. It has been observed that it is not in accord with Mark's style and may be due to liturgical influence. The forgiveness of sins and the celebration of the Eucharist would have been associated at an early date.

Another important text for the teaching on forgiveness is the Lord's Prayer. It is found both in Matthew

(6:9-13) and in Luke (11:2-4), the latter in a much shorter form. The Matthean form exposes more forcefully the use of the prayer in the Christian community. In the fifth petition we read: "forgive us the wrong we have done as we forgive those who wrong us" (6:12). Note that when Christians ask God to forgive them as they forgive others, the "as" is not intended to suggest exact proportion, as though God's forgiveness were measured by man's. It means simply that God forgives when man forgives. Again, this does not mean that God's forgiveness is conditional. Rather, God's forgiveness, which always is present, does not reach the heart of the man who harbors enmity toward his brother. By closing himself to his brother, he closes himself to God's forgiveness.

Matthew has an additional saying of Jesus attached to the end of the Our Father that allows us to see the evangelist's interpretation of the prayer: "If you forgive the faults of others, your heavenly Father will forgive you yours. If you do not forgive others, neither will your Father forgive you" (6:14-15). By adding this saying here, Matthew has given particular stress to that one petition in the prayer.

But what is behind this emphasis on mutual forgiveness? The likely solution is a bit complex, consisting of several elements, but it is worth considering. The Our Father was used early in the liturgy, just as it occupies a prominent place today in our celebration of the Eucharist. As such, it was recited only by those who had accepted Jesus Christ. In the early Church, not even those who were taking instructions were allowed to recite it. It was a decidedly community prayer.

Moreover, in Matthew's version, as has been shown by the form of the Greek verbs used, the stress in all the petitions is on the eschatological community, that is, on the community as it will be in the end-time when the fullness of union with the Father will be achieved. The petitions of the prayer are directed to this end-time. In this light, the community is, of course, a sinless community, fully forgiven of their sins by the Father and by each other, a situation that is the object of the fifth petition. The two verses added by Matthew highlight this final state of forgiveness.

A consideration of Matthew 18:15-20 will help further in understanding this preoccupation. The whole of chapter 18 has been called the community discourse, since it deals exclusively with the Christian community in its members' relations with one another. This particular section, vv. 15-20, deals with fraternal correction, the possible excommunication of the sinner, the community's power to bind and loose, and community prayer. In the last saying, Jesus enunciates the principle that "if two of you join your voices on earth to pray for anything whatever, it shall be granted you by my Father in heaven" (18:19). By joining this saying to the preceding section on fraternal correction, which includes the rejection by the Church of the unrepentant sinner, Matthew is implying that the power of community prayer is predicated on the community's sinlessness. "Thus the prayer of the messianic community presupposes a mutually forgiven community" (K. Stendahl). It is the same reason why the evangelist has added the sayings on forgiveness to the Our Father. "In essence it is an assertion that the right to utter this prayer belonged only to a mutually reconciled, and therefore, sinless, community" (J. Murphy-O'Connor).

In making some application of all these threads of thought, we can say that in the celebration of the Eucharistic liturgy, we are anticipating the eschatological union with the Father through Jesus Christ. As a sign of that union, we recite, at the conclusion of the great Eucharistic prayer, the eschatological prayer, the Our Father. In reciting it, we are minded of our need for mutual forgiveness if we are to share fully in the grace of that union. The prayer is followed then by the reception of the Eucharistic Lord who thus fulfills in a perfect way His promise to the community, "Where two or three are gathered in my name, there am I in their midst" (Matthew 18:20).

The New Testament doctrine on forgiveness of sins thus brings to fulfillment the Old Testament teaching. Now both God and man are caught up in the world of salvation: God forgiving man, and man forgiving his brother. Always, however, as in the Old Testament, the initiative is God's. By extending His forgiving love to man through the victory over sin won by Jesus Christ, He has made it possible for man to open his heart to his fellowman. Moreover, within the Christian community itself, this forgiveness creates an eschatological community that already is able to savor the final union with the Father. In the Eucharistic assembly, which is and must be a forgiving and forgiven assembly, the union reaches a dramatic climax through the presence of and communion with the risen Lord.

Sources

References used in the text, in the order in which they appear:

Gottfried Quell, *"Hamartanō,"* in *Theological Dictionary of the New Testament,* (G. Kittel, ed.), Vol. I, translated by G. Bromiley, Grand Rapids, 1964.

Paul Ricoeur, quoted by A. Gelin in *Sin in the Bible,* New York, 1964.

Leo Scheffczyk, "The Meaning of Christ's Parousia for the Salvation of Man and the Cosmos," in *The Christian and the World, Readings in Theology,* New York, 1965.

Gunther Bornkamm, *Jesus of Nazareth,* New York, 1960.

Piet Schoonenberg, "Sin," in *Sacramentum Mundi*, (K. Rahner, S.J., ed.), Vol. VI, New York, 1970.

Joseph Fitzmyer, S.J., "The Letter to the Romans," in *Jerome Biblical Commentary*, (R. E. Brown, S.S., J. A. Fitzmyer, S.J., R. E. Murphy, O. Carm., eds.), Englewood Cliffs, 1968.

Thomas Worden, "The Remission of Sins," in *Sacraments in Scripture*, (T. Worden, ed.), Springfield, 1966.

Kevin O'Shea, "The Reality of Sin: A Theological and Pastoral Critique," in *The Mystery of Sin and Forgiveness*, (M. J. Taylor, S.J., ed.), Staten Island, 1971.

C. F. D. Moule, *Man and Nature in the New Testament*, Philadelphia, 1967.

Piet Smulders, S.J., "Evolution and Original Sin," in *The Mystery of Sin and Forgiveness*, (M. J. Taylor, S.J., ed.), Staten Island, 1971.

Piet Schoonenberg, S.J., "Original Sin and Man's Situation," in *The Mystery of Sin and Forgiveness*, (M. J. Taylor, S.J., ed.), Staten Island, 1971.

Krister Stendahl, quoted by J. Murphy-O'Connor, O.P., "Sin and Community in the New Testament," in *Sin and Repentance,* (D. O'Callaghan, ed.), Staten Island, 1967.

Krister Stendahl, "Matthew," in *Peake's Commentary on the Bible,* (M. Black, H. H. Rowley, eds.), London, 1962.

Jerome Murphy-O'Connor, O.P., "Sin and Community in the New Testament," in *Sin and Repentance,* (D. O'Callaghan, ed.), Staten Island, 1967.

Further Reading

The following brief bibliography will provide more detailed information on various aspects of sin.

A. Gelin, A. Descamps, *Sin in the Bible,* Desclee, New York, 1964. A survey of the notion of sin in both the Old and New Testaments, with a much greater concentration on the latter.

P. Schoonenberg, S.J., *Man and Sin,* University of Notre Dame Press, 1965. A thorough and scholarly study of the theological aspects of sin.

A.-M. Dubarle, O.P., *The Biblical Doctrine of Original Sin,* Herder and Herder, New York, 1964. A scholarly study of the biblical teaching on original sin.

D. O'Callaghan (ed.), *Sin and Repentance,* Alba House, Staten Island, 1967. A collection of ten essays on the subject by some leading Irish and English scholars.

M. J. Taylor, S.J. (ed.), *The Mystery of Sin and Forgiveness,* Alba House, Staten Island, 1971. A collection of five essays on sin, five on forgiveness, and four on original sin by scholars from many countries.

T. Worden (ed.), *Sacraments in Scripture,* Templegate, Springfield, Ill., 1966. These essays, by European scholars, include four on various aspects of sin.

C. Luke Salm, F.S.C. (ed.), *Readings in Biblical Morality,* Prentice-Hall, Englewood Cliffs, 1967. Twelve essays on a variety of themes dealing with morality.